M000307586

HEATHEN DAYS

The Buncombe Collection
Books by H. L. Mencken

A Second Mencken Chrestomathy: A New Selection from the Writings of America's Legendary Editor, Critic, and Wit
Selected, revised, and annotated by the author
Edited and with an introduction by Terry Teachout

Thirty-five Years of Newspaper Work: A Memoir by H. L. Mencken
Edited by Fred Hobson, Vincent Fitzpatrick, and Bradford Jacobs

Happy Days: 1880–1892

Newspaper Days: 1899–1906

Heathen Days: 1890–1936

Prejudices: A Selection
Selected and with an introduction by James T. Farrell

Treatise on the Gods

On Politics: A Carnival of Buncombe

Minority Report

HEATHEN DAYS

1890-1936

H. L. MENCKEN

The Johns Hopkins University Press
Baltimore

Some of these chapters have appeared, either wholly or in part, in the *New Yorker*, and one, "Downfall of a Revolutionary," was first published in *Esquire*. The author offers his thanks to the editors of these magazines for permission to reprint them.

© 1941, 1942, 1943 by Alfred A. Knopf, Inc.
All rights reserved. Published 2006
Printed in the United States of America on acid-free paper

Originally published in a hardcover edition by Alfred A. Knopf, Inc.
Published by arrangement with Alfred A. Knopf, Inc.
Maryland Paperback Bookshelf edition, 1996
The Buncombe Collection, 2006
9 8 7 6 5 4 3 2 1

The Johns Hopkins University Press
2715 North Charles Street
Baltimore, Maryland 21218-4363
www.press.jhu.edu

The Buncombe Collection ISBN 0-8018-8532-9 (pbk.: alk. paper)

The Library of Congress has cataloged the 1996 edition of this book as follows:

Mencken, H. L. (Henry Louis), 1880–1956.
Heathen days, 1890–1936 / H. L. Mencken.—Maryland paperback bookshelf ed.
p. cm.—(Maryland paperback bookshelf)
Originally published : New York : Knopf, 1943.
ISBN 0-8018-5339-7 (alk. paper)
1. Mencken, H. L. (Henry Louis), 1880–1956—Biography. 2. Authors, American—20th century—Biography. 3. Journalists—United States—Biography. I. Title. II. Series.
PS3525.E43Z446 1996
818'.5209—dc20
[B]

95-53071

A catalog record for this book is available from the British Library.

Frontispiece: Courtesy of the Enoch Pratt Free Library.

TABLE OF

CONTENTS

PREFACE

When I finished " Happy Days " in August, 1939, anchored to an Underwood Noiseless Portable in the lovely Summer home of Dr. and Mrs. Frederic M. Hanes, high up in the North Carolina mountains, it would have astonished me unfeignedly if one of the native necromancers had dropped in from a neighboring Alp and told me that two similar volumes would follow it. I had had a grand time doing the book, but it seemed to me that one dose of my *curriculum vitae* was enough for posterity, and with the troubles of the teens peeping round the corner in my memory, I was rather glad to be shet of the subject. It soon appeared, however, that I was in the hands of higher powers, some of them supernatural but most of them merely human. The latter were customers who began writing in suggesting that I do a companion volume on my early newspaper adventures, and in a little while I had so far succumbed to their blarney that a couple of chapters thereof were sketched out. This was in 1940. The project occupied me off and on during the year, but in the main I worked on my "New Dictionary of Quotations," and when 1941 dawned "Newspaper Days" was still only a fragment. I thereupon decided, heroically but idiotically, to jam through both books together, and the result was that I landed in hospital in April, with the dictionary finished but "Newspaper Days" yet very far short of it. After I got out of their animal-house the resurrection men ordered me to take a holiday, and I went to Cuba by sea — probably my last ocean trip on this earth. I spent a couple of lazy weeks in Havana and its environs, hearing some excellent music, watching (and getting converted to) the cavortings of a Russian ballet company, and putting away large quantities of the nourishing Cuban victuals. When I got back to Baltimore I had so far recovered that I had a sudden burst of energy, and was soon knocking off what remained of "Newspaper Days" at the rate of 3,000 words a day — my all-time high for sustained writing. The MS. was in the hands of the Knopfs by June 18, and on June 24 I was writing to Blanche: "I note your acceptance of 'Newspaper Days.' It is naturally gratifying to a young author."

The present volume is a kind of by-product of the burst of energy just mentioned. When I came to the end of the period marked off for "Newspaper Days," I simply could not stop, but kept on going until I had accumulated four or five redundant chapters. When wind of these reached Harold W. Ross, the alert editor of the *New Yorker*, he collared them for his instructive weekly, and urged me to go on to more. When "Newspaper Days" came out in the Autumn of 1941 there was further heat from customers, and even a few whiffs from reviewers, so the present volume gradually and inevitably took form. It covers a wider range of time than either of its predecessors, for in it I have included a couple of chapters that belong to my *Erinnerungen aus dem fröhlichen Bubenleben* but somehow failed to fit into "Happy Days," and on the other end I bring it down to 1936. But there is no continuity in it, and none was attempted. It is simply a series of random reminiscences, not always photographically precise, of a life that, on the whole, has been very busy and excessively pleasant. Like any other man I have had my disasters and my miseries, and like any other author I have suffered from recurrent depressions and despairs, but taking one year with another I have had a fine time of it in this vale of sorrow, and no call to envy any man. Indeed, I seem to have been born without any capacity for envy, and to the fact, no doubt, is due a large part of my habitual tranquility, not to say complacency. But in part that contentment of spirit is due also to a kind of caginess that has dissuaded me, at all stages of my life, from attempting enterprises clearly beyond my power. Sticking always to what I could do with reasonable comfort, I have escaped the pains of complete bafflement, and thus have no motive, whether Freudian or other, for begrudging the other fellow his competence. Indeed, I simply can't imagine competence as anything save admirable, for it is very rare in this world, and especially in this great Republic, and those who have it in some measure, in any art or craft from adultery to zoölogy, are the only human beings I can think of who will be worth the oil it will take to fry them in Hell.

Despite my two previous miscalculations, this third volume of my more or less accurate memories will probably be my last, for I begin to be impressed, at sixty-two, with the cogency of the Chinese warning that "it is later than you think"; and if I actually do any more dredging out of the past it will undoubtedly be in a more chastened and scientific mood. The hereditary pedant in me has made me a diligent conservator of records, and in the files in my cellar are enough of them to entertain a whole herd of nascent Ph.D.'s — records of forty-three years on newspapers, of forty as a writer of books, of twenty-five as a reviewer, of twenty as a magazine editor. These vocations have overlapped, but they have also intermingled, and some of my chronicles are thus rather complicated. When I was engaged a little while back in trying to get some order into them, I was struck by the thought that every man given over professionally to hearing and seeing things ought to be allowed two lives — one to hear and see and the other to set down what he has heard and seen. But inasmuch as no such thought seems to have occurred to the Creator of the species, I am doomed to an inevitable but sorry compromise. Having now done three volumes of my recollections, I shall turn away from the past for a while and devote myself to hearing and seeing some more. I can only say of the present volume, as I said of its two predecessors, that it is not sober history but yarning, and is thus devoid of any purpose save to entertain. If it fails there it is a flop indeed. The title, alas, comes a good deal short of satisfying me. In its provisional or studio form I thought of the book as "Miscellaneous Days," for it covers a long period and shows me at ages ranging from the agonies of nonage to the beginnings of senility. But there were objections to "Miscellaneous Days" that need not be gone into here, so I began concocting various other titles, all of them bad — "Busy Days," "Gaudy Days," "Red-Letter Days," "Assiduous Days," and so on. Finally, I hit on "Heathen Days," which is probably worse than any of them. The precisely right title would be "Happy Days III," just as the precisely right title for "Newspaper Days" was "Happy Days II," but it is now too late to undo the mistake I made in 1941.

PREFACE

In my efforts to keep down my errors in names, dates and other facts to a reasonable minimum I have thrown myself on the kindness of several friends with better memories than my own — especially, George Jean Nathan, my former associate in many a gay enterprise; A. H. McDannald, my companion in one that is herein described at some length; Dr. Paul de Kruif, a partner in another; and Richard J. Beamish, now a member of the Public Utility Commission of Pennsylvania, but formerly a reporter as I was, and a much better one. Most of all I owe thanks to another old colleague and friend — Edgar Ellis, librarian of the Baltimore *Sunpapers*. Mr. Ellis has not only built up a newspaper morgue of the first class; he has also learned how to find his way about in it, so that its veriest scrap of information is immediately at his hand. I called on him for help at least two dozen times while the pages following were in progress, and not once did he fail me. Without his aid, always generously given, my record would show a great many more stretchers than now adorn it.

BALTIMORE, 1942. H. L. M.

HEATHEN DAYS

I

DOWNFALL

OF A REVOLUTIONARY

[*1890*]

OF all the eminent characters who flourished in the West Baltimore of my infancy, the one most venerated by the boys of my generation was Hoggie Unglebower, an uncouth youth whose empire and influence, radiating out from an humble stable in the alley which ran behind our house in Hollins street, covered altogether an area of at least half a square mile. No storekeeper of that time and place was better known, whether for good or for evil, nor any cop, however heinous, nor any ma'am in the public school up Hollins street hill, nor bad nigger in Vincent alley, nor blind man in practice at Hollins market. Between the longitude of the market and the wilderness of Steuart's Hill, all through a chunk of territory four or five blocks thick, he was a hero to every boy above the age of seven.

The reader of today, soaked in the Freudian sewage for so many years, will assume at once, I suppose, that Hoggie must have been a Lothario, and his headquarters a seraglio. Nothing could have been further from the truth. He was actually almost a Trappist in his glandular life, and his hormones never gave him any visible trouble until much later on, as I shall show in due course. In the days of his greatest glory his view of all human females was predominantly disdainful, but it never led him to use them wickedly, or even impolitely. When a hired girl issued into the alley to flag a rag-and-bone man or hunt for a lost garbage box he would whistle at her satirically and shout "Ah, there!" but at the same time he always took off his hat. To women of greater age and station he was courteous to an extreme degree, and when he visited a neighboring dwelling with his terriers to purge it of rats he always wiped his feet at the back door, and never failed to address the lady of the house as Ma'am.

No, Hoggie was not carnal in the Catechism sense, and I incline to think that that was one of the reasons all the boys so greatly respected him. The male infantry of today, debauched by Progressive Education and the sex hygiene quackery, are said to be adepts at the arts of love before they are more than half house-broken, but that was certainly not true in my time. The boys of that Mousterian generation, until adolescence came down upon them, regarded girls with frank aversion, and had as little truck with them as with cats or cops. It is, of course, a fact that the probable delights of amour were occasionally discussed, but it was always vaguely and with a considerable uneasiness, for any move to put a concrete project into effect would have involved a close approach to females, and that was never done if it could be helped. What made Hoggie a personage was nothing in that line; it was mainly, and perhaps even only, his successful and notorious resistance to the doctrine that cleanliness is next to godliness.

In his father's stable he led the life dreamed of as ideal by all normal boys, then, now, and forever. No one, it appeared, had any authority (at all events any authority that he recognized) to make him comb his hair, or brush his clothes, or shine his shoes, or wash behind the ears. He wallowed there day in and day out, including especially Sundays, in such slops as every normal boy longs to own, but is seldom permitted to have. Preferring the society of horses and dogs to that of men, he lived among them freely and unashamedly, sleeping with them, eating with them, and sharing his confidences with them. He got his hair cut when he damned well pleased, and it wasn't often. Hating neckties, he never wore them. When he thirsted, he drank from the end of the stable hose, and if anyone stopped to gape at him he squeezed the hose (which was old, soft and full of holes) and sent a fine stream into the gaper's eye.

In brief, a magnificent specimen of Natural Man, somehow surviving unscathed every corruption of an effete and pusillanimous civilization. He came of a bourgeois family and had been to school, but had fought off successfully every effort to denaturize him. His days were busy, and full of enterprises that, to us boys, were important, difficult and romantic. He was the architect, builder and navigator of the largest and fastest double-decker sleds known in West Baltimore, and probably the best repairer of boys' wagons ever seen in Christendom. He knew how to knock a barrel to pieces without splitting any of the staves, and how to put it together again. He could teach tricks to horses, and had so far mastered their vocabulary of whinnies and pawings that he carried on long conversations with them, often laughing at their pawky humor. He was a dog doctor of great gifts, and kept a large stock of medicines for his patients on a shelf in the stable. To cops, despite all their clubs, handcuffs and sidearms, he presented a calm and unflickering eye, and they had a high respect for him, for when he went to the aid of one who was overwhelmed by a passel of bad niggers, the bad niggers lost consciousness almost instantly, and awoke in the watch-house with huge bumps on their heads. Hoggie, disdaining firearms, did his fighting with clubs, and had an arsenal of them ready to hand — little ones for light jobs, and thick, warty shillalahs for really earnest work. When he came down upon a skull something gave way, and it was never Hoggie or his weapon.

He was the best dog-trainer for miles around, and could transfer even the sorriest mutt into a competent ratter. For this purpose he liked to have them young; indeed, he preferred to begin on them as soon as their eyes were open. At that age, of course, they were no match for actual rats, and even the more active sort of mice had the edge on them. To equalize the odds, Hoggie would catch infant rats in a trap, pull their teeth with a pair of pliers, and then throw them into a barrel with a couple of his pupils. As the latter gained in strength and technique, he would test them with rats of gradually larger growth, retaining at first one tooth each, and then two, and then four or five, and finally a whole set, upper and lower. Now and then a freshman was badly mauled in these exercises, but Hoggie did not despair, for he knew that any sort of educational process was bound to be painful, and he preferred the hard way for dogs as for men. His graduates were all recognized virtuosi. One day he let me go along as he took one to a hay-and-feed warehouse for a final examination. The candidate was only a spindly black-and-tan, but within three minutes by the watch he had unearthed, run down and killed a whole bucket of rats, some of them of the fearsome sewer variety, with fangs two inches long.

Hoggie admired dogs, and was admired by them in turn, though his medicating of them ran to heroic measures. His usual prescription for the common run of canine malaises was the better part of half a pound of Glauber's salts. The colored quacks who practised a Dahomeyan farriery in Reveille's livery stable down the street hesitated to give so large a dose to anything short of a cart horse, but Hoggie believed that it was foolish to temporize with disease, and proved it by curing most of his patients. He was also adept at surgery, and could point to at least a dozen dogs that he had treated successfully for broken bones. He sutured the lacerations that followed dog-fights with the thick, black thread used by shoemakers, and always waxed it carefully before setting to work. He was, I believe, the first canine dentist ever in practice in Baltimore; to this day, in fact, they are rare. He pulled the damaged teeth of his patients with the same pair of pliers that he employed to prepare rats for his academy, and sometimes he had to pull very hard. I heard him say once that most dogs, like most human beings, were born with too many teeth, and that getting rid of half a dozen or so toned up their systems and improved their dispositions.

No one that I ever heard of approached him in the delicate art of trimming puppies' tails. His technique was of the whirlwind variety: the tail was off before the puppy had a chance to be alarmed. In my earliest days he had a formidable rival in old Julius, an Aframerican *mohel* with headquarters in Reveille's stable, but as the years passed he gobbled all of Julius's practice, and in the end his mastery was admitted by everyone. In that era the different breeds of dogs in vogue nearly all wore their tails clipped, so Hoggie was kept busy. I have seen him knock off six or eight of an afternoon, with the whole Hollins-street gang for a gallery. Our own dogs, from the early eighties onward to the middle nineties, all passed through his hands, and every one of them was friendly to him afterward, and wagged its stump whenever it encountered him. He also treated dogs when they took to nibbling grass in the yard or showed other signs of indisposition — always with that massive dose of Glauber's salts as a starter. He had plenty of other medicines, and used them freely on occasion, but he depended mainly on the Glauber's salts, just as Dr. Wiley, our family doctor, depended on castor oil.

Hoggie's incurable boyishness was shown by the fact that, for all his fondness for horses and dogs, he hated cats with a blind and implacable hatred, and spent a great deal of his time tracking them down and executing them. There was a time, indeed, when his chronic war upon them aroused some ill-will in the neighborhood — but not, of course, among the boys. What was done about it I forget, but for a while he locked himself in his stable, and refused to have any truck with human society. Even the cops were given to understand that their room was preferred to their company. But then a stray cat scratched a baby down the block, and under cover of the ensuing uproar Hoggie emerged from his solitude, and resumed his crusade. I well recall the day when, as a gesture of triumph, he threw eight dead cats into the alley in one lot, and got into a row with the street cleaner who had to haul them away. The street cleaner, it appeared, held that a person engaged in such wholesale slaughters should dispose of his own dead, and not dump them on public officials. He cited the example of the hotels which carted off their own garbage, and that of the candy factory down the alley which kept a wagon to handle its own boiler ashes, but Hoggie refused to allow any weight to the argument. So far as he was concerned, he said, the cats could lie in the alley until the Judgment Day, along with the rats that he heaved out almost daily — the melancholy refuse of his college for puppies. The street cleaner muttered a while longer and threatened several times to submit the whole matter to Murphy the cop, but in the end he loaded the cats upon his cart, and during the weeks that followed he loaded many others. Until a fresh generation of kittens worked its way in from Hollins market, the Union Square neighborhood was almost as bare of *Felidae* as Greenland. A few, of course, survived in houses, but they were kept as closely penned as canary birds.

The boys of the Hollins-street gang believed, like well-educated American boys everywhere else, that cats had nine lives, but Hoggie dissented. He admitted freely that no cat within his experience ever had so little as one life, but he insisted that his researches indicated that five was the limit. Indeed, it was only battle-scarred old Toms who went even that far: the average free-lance cat, depleted by its wandering, precarious life, was disposed of finally after being killed three or four times. One day the alley metaphysician, Old Wesley, undertook to point out a possible statistical fallacy in this doctrine. What evidence was there, he demanded, that the Toms which Hoggie killed five times had not been killed four times before by other executioners, thus making up the classical nine? This argument, rather to the astonishment of his listening admirers, floored Hoggie completely. The louder he howled against it, the more he became confused and out of temper, and in the end he was reduced to the sorry expedient of denouncing Wesley as a sassy nigger, and threatening to set the medical students on him. His failure in the debate, and above all his resort to what amounted to forensic blackmail, lowered his stock with the boys of Hollins street, but not for long. In a little while he recovered face gloriously by staging, in the privacy of his stable, a dog-fight that went down into history as the most gory ever seen in West Baltimore.

Despite his unhappy encounter with Old Wesley, he was commonly on good terms with the colored people who lived in the alley, and exercised a general jurisdiction over them, milder and more understanding than that of the cops. They had a high respect for him, and went to him in their troubles, though in his practice as dog-doctor and cat-and-rat exterminator he was uncomfortably close to a medical student. He did not hold himself out as skilled at human medicine, but the bottles he kept for dosing dogs were at the disposal of any blackamoor who wanted to try them, and many professed to be benefited. In particular, the liniment he used on dogs run over by carts was said to be very efficacious against rheumatoid afflictions in *Anthropoidea.* Once he scared off all his Aframerican patients by stuffing a dead cat with oats, and using black shoe-buttons for its eyes. This gruesome object, while it remained on exhibition, kept all the colored people out of his stable, though we white boys thought it was very nobby. It didn't last long, for the huge, ferocious rats of Hollins market quickly heard of it, and one night they rushed the stable and devoured it, eyes and all. All that remained of it the next morning was a carriage-bolt that Hoggie had employed to counteract the flaccidity of the oats.

His downfall I can place with reasonable accuracy in the year 1890, when I was ten years old and he must have been about twenty-two or three. One afternoon in Summer, on my way to Reveille's livery stable to visit my father's horse, John, who was laid up with epizootic, I encountered Hoggie at the corner of Baltimore street in such vestments that I stopped dead in my tracks, and gaped at him as if he had been a cop in motley or a two-headed boy. He had on a brand-new suit of store clothes, golden brown in color, and wore a pair of the immense yellow shoes then in fashion — as wide, almost, as a street-car at the ball of the foot, but stretched out to a long point at the toe. On his head was a cart-wheel straw hat with a brim at least six inches deep, and a gorgeous red-and-white ribbon. His collar, which was of fresh celluloid, rose above a boiled shirt that gleamed like snow on the Alps, and around it he wore a bright green four-in-hand tie, with the ends tucked over to expose a stud that glittered like a diamond, but was no doubt something else. He was shaved so closely that his neck and chin were criss-crossed with red gashes, and the rest of his face was a brilliant vermilion. Finally, and most amazing of all, his hair — at least such of it as I could see below his hat — was cropped to its roots according to the best technique of Barber Lehnert. As I passed him, I caught a gust of Jockey Club scent, familiar to me as the special favorite of our current hired girl. I was so astounded that I passed him without greeting him, staring foolishly. He paid no attention to me, but stalked along painfully, like a man in a barrel. I spread the news over the neighborhood, and Hoggie's secret quickly leaked out.

He had succumbed at last, after all his years of outlawry, to one of the most conventional of human weaknesses: he had fallen in love. The ancient psychosis that had floored and made a mock of Marc Antony, Dante and Goethe — but *not* Shakespeare, Napoleon Bonaparte or George Washington — had now fetched him too. Some inconsiderable and probably pie-faced slip of a girl, name unknown, had collared him, tamed him, and made of him the dreadful popinjay that I had seen. The rest of the pathetic story follows classical lines, and is soon told. Hoggie disappeared from his stable, and was reported to be occupying a bedroom in the Unglebower family home, and actually eating at table. In a little while he vanished altogether, and reports came in that he was married to the lady, living in far Northwest Baltimore, and at work as a horse-car driver. That was the last I ever heard of him.

II

MEMOIRS OF THE

STABLE

[*1891*]

Horses, taking one with another, are supposed to be the stupidest creatures (forgetting, of course, horse-lovers) within the confines of our Christian civilization, but there are naturally some exceptions, and they probably include the whole race of Shetland ponies. During the interminable epoch stretching from my eleventh year to my fourteenth I was on confidential terms with such a pony, and came to have a very high opinion of his sagacity. As the phrase ran in those days, he was as sharp as a trap, and also excessively immoral. The last word, I should say at once, I do not use in the Puritan or Freudian sense, for Frank was a gelding; what I seek to convey is simply the idea that he was also a cheat, a rogue and a scoundrel. Nearly all his waking hours were given over to deceiving and afflicting my brother Charlie and me. He bit us, he kicked us, he stepped on our toes, he crowded us against the walls of his stall, and he sneezed in our faces, and in the intervals he tried to alarm us by running away, or by playing sick or dead. Nevertheless, we loved him, and mixed with our affection there was a great deal of sincere admiration.

Where he was bred we never heard, and, boy-like, did not inquire. One day in the Autumn of 1891 a couple of carpenters appeared in Hollins street and began to throw up a miniature stable at the end of the long backyard, and by the time they got the roof on Frank was in it, along with a yellow go-cart, a tabloid buggy with fringe around its top, a couple of sets of harness, and a saddle. It soon turned out that there was not room enough in the stable for both the go-cart and the buggy, so the buggy was moved to Reveille's livery-stable two blocks away, where my father's horse John was in residence. Simultaneously, a colored intern was brought in from the same place to instruct Charlie and me in the principles of his art, for we were told that we were to have the honor of caring for Frank. Inasmuch as we had been hanging about stables since infancy, watching the blackamoors at their work, this hint that we needed tutelage rather affronted us, but we were so delighted by the privilege of becoming hostlers — the dream of every American boy in that horsy age — that we let it pass, and only too soon we learned that there was a great deal more to servicing a Shetland pony than could be picked up by watching blackamoors service full-grown horses.

Charlie, I believe, got the first kick, but I got the first bite. It was delivered with sly suddenness on the second morning after the intern from Reveille's had graduated me *cum laude* and gone back to his regular job. He had cautioned me that, in currying any sort of horse it was necessary to pay particular heed to the belly, for it tended to pick up contamination from the stall litter, and he had added the warning that the belly was a sensitive area, and must be tackled gently. I was gentle enough, goodness knows, but Frank, as I was soon to learn, objected to any sort of currying whatsoever, top or bottom, and so, when I stooped down to reach under his hull — he was only nine hands high at the withers — he fetched me a good nip in the seat of my pants. My reaction was that of a coiled spring of high tension, and it was thus hardly more than a split second before I was out in the yard, rubbing my backside with both hands. When I tell you that Frank laughed you will, of course, set me down a nature-faker; all the same, I tell you that Frank laughed. I could see him through the window above his feed-trough, and there were all the indubitable signs — the head thrown back, the mouth open, the lips retracted, the teeth shining, the tears running down both cheeks. I could even hear a sound like a chuckle. Thereafter I never consciously exposed my caboose to him, but time and again he caught me unawares, and once he gave me a nip so severe that the scar remains to this day. Whenever I get to hospital — which is only too often in these later years — the sportive young doctors enter it upon their chart as a war wound.

Frank quickly developed a really marvelous technic of escape. He had a box-stall that, considering his size, was roomy, and Charlie and I kept it so clean that the hostlers from all the other stables in the alley would drop in to admire it. There was a frame of soft red clay to ease his forefeet, and a large piece of rock-salt to entertain him on lazy afternoons. He got hearty meals of substantial horse-victuals three times a day, and in cold weather the water used to mix his mill-feed was always warm. Through the window above his trough he could look out into the yard, and a section of it about twenty feet square was fenced off to give him a paddock. In this paddock he was free to disport a couple of hours every day, save only when there was snow on the ground. But when he was in it he devoted most of his time to hanging his head over the paling-fence, lusting for the regions beyond. Just out of his reach was a peach tree, and beyond it a pear tree, both still young and tender. One fine Spring day, with both trees burgeoning, he somehow cracked the puzzle of the catch on the paddock gate, and by the time he was discovered he had eaten all the bark off the peach tree, from the ground to a height of four feet. Charlie and I found it hard to blame him, for we liked the peach gum ourselves and often chewed it, flies and all, but my mother wept when the tree died, and the paddock gate was outfitted with an iron bar and two chains.

Frank never got through it again — that is, by his own effort. But one day, when a feeble-minded hired girl left it open, he was in the yard instantly and made a killing that still lives in the family tradition. Rather curiously, he did not molest the pear tree, but by the time he was chased back to his own ground he had devoured a bed of petunias, all my mother's best dahlias, the better part of a grape vine, and the whole of my father's mint patch. I have been told by eminent horse-lovers that horses never touch mint, but I am here dealing, not with a horse, but with a Shetland pony. Frank gradually acquired many other strange appetites — for example, for ice cream. Every time it was on tap in the house he would smell it and begin to stamp and whinny, and in the end it became the custom to give him whatever happened to be left. Once, when the hired girl got salt into it and the whole batch was spoiled, he devoured all of it — probably a gallon and a half — and then drank two buckets of water. He also ate oranges (skin and all), bananas (spitting out the skin), grapes, asparagus and sauerkraut. One day Charlie tried him with a slab of rat-trap cheese, but he refused it. Another day Charlie gave him a piece of plug tobacco wrapped in a cabbage leaf, but again without success. This last trick, in fact, offended him and he sought revenge at once. When he bit through the cabbage into the tobacco he gave a sudden and violent cough, and the plug hit Charlie in the eye.

When we were in the country in Summer Frank had my father's horse John for a stable-mate, and they got on together well enough, though it was plain to see that Frank regarded John as an idiot. This was a reasonable judgment, for John, who was a trotter, was actually very backward mentally, and could be easily scared. Whenever the two were in pasture together Frank would alarm John by bearing down upon him at a gallop, as if about to leap over him. This would set John to running away, and Frank would pursue him all over the pasture, whinnying and laughing. John himself could no more laugh than he could read and write. He was a tall, slim sorrel with a long, narrow head, and was so stupid that he even showed no pride in his speed, which was considerable. Life to him was a gloomy business, and he was often in the hands of horse-doctors. If there was a stone on the road he always picked it up, and when we were in the country and Charlie and I had charge of him we never bedded him down for the night without investigating his frogs. In the course of an average Summer we recovered at least twenty nails from them, not to mention burrs and splinters. Like most valetudinarians he lived to a great age. After my father's death we sold him to an animal show that had Winter quarters in Baltimore, and he spent his last years as a sort of companion to a herd of trained zebras. The zebras, I heard, had a lot of fun with him.

One night, an hour or so after midnight, there was a dreadful kicking and grunting in our stable in the country, and my father and Charlie and I turned out to inquire into it. We found John standing in the middle of his box-stall in a pitiable state of mind, his coat ruffled and his eyes staring. Frank, next door, was apparently sleeping soundly. We examined John from head to foot, but could find nothing wrong, so we contented ourselves with giving him a couple of random doses from his enormous armamentarium of medicine bottles, and talking to him in soothing tones. He seemed quite all right in the morning, and my father drove him to and from town, but that night there was another hullabaloo in the stable, and we had to turn out again. On the day following John was put to grass and Charlie and I went for a colored horse-doctor in Cross Keys, a nearby village. He advised us to throw away all of John's medicines, and prescribed instead a mild course of condition powders, with a handful of flaxseed once a day. This was begun instantly, but that night the same dreadful noises came from the stable, and again the night following, and again the night after that, and so on for a week. Two or three other horse-doctors were called in during that time, but they were all baffled, and John took to looking seedy and even mangy. Meanwhile, my father began to suffer seriously from the interruptions to his sleep, and talked wildly of having the poor horse shot and his carcass sent to a glue-factory. Also, he began to discover unpleasant weaknesses in his old friend Herman Ellis, from whom John had been bought. Ellis, hitherto, had been held up to Charlie and me as a model, but now it appeared that he drank too much, kept two sets of books, was a Methodist, and ought to be expelled from the Freemasons.

Charlie and I, talking the business over at length, came to the conclusion eventually that there must be more to it than met the eye, and so decided to keep watch at the stable. There was already floating through our minds, I think, some suspicion of Frank, for we were at pains to prevent him learning what we were up to. At our bedtime we sneaked into the carriage-house on tiptoe, and there made ourselves bunks in the family dayton-wagon. We were soon sound asleep, but at the usual time we were aroused by a great clomping and banging in the stalls adjoining, and turned out to take a stealthy look. It was a moonlight night, and enough of the gentle glare was filtering into the stable to give us an excellent view. What we saw scarcely surprised us. All the uproar, we discovered, was being made by Frank, not by John. Frank was having a whale of a time flinging his heels against the sides of his stall. The noise plainly delighted him, and he was laughing gaily. Presently poor John, waking in alarm, leaped to his feet and began to tremble. At this Frank gave a couple of final clouts, and then lay down calmly and went to sleep — or, at all events, appeared to. But John, trying with his limp mind to make out what was afoot, kept on trembling, and was, in fact, still half scared to death when we announced our presence and tried to comfort him.

My father had arrived by this time, his slippers flapping, his suspenders hanging loose and blood in his eye, and we soon made him understand what had happened. His only comment was "Well, I'll be durned!" repeated twenty or thirty times. We soon had a bridle on Frank, with a strap rigged from it to his left hind leg, and if he tried any more kicking that night he knocked himself down, which was certainly no more than he deserved. But we heard no more noise, nor was there any the next night, or the next, or the next. After a week we removed the strap, and then sat up again to see what would happen. But nothing happened, for Frank had learned his lesson. At some time or other while the strap was on, I suppose, he had tried a kick — and gone head over heels in his stall. He was, as I have said, a smart fellow, and there was never any need to teach him the same thing twice. Thereafter, until the end of the Summer, he let poor John sleep in peace. My father fired all the horse-doctors, white and black, and threw out all their remedies. John recovered quickly, and a little while later did a mile on the Pimlico road in 2.17½ — not a bad record, for he was pulling a steel-tired buggy with my father and me in it, and the road was far from level.

In that same stable, the next Summer, Frank indulged himself in a jape which came near costing him his life. To recount it I must describe briefly the lay-out of the place. He inhabited a box-stall with a low wall, and in that wall was a door fastened by a movable wooden cleat. He was in the habit of hanging his head over the door, and drooling lubriciously, while Charlie and I were preparing his feed. This feed came down from the hayloft through a chute that emptied into a large wooden trough, and he often saw us start the feed by pulling out a paddle in the chute. One night either Charlie or I neglected to fasten the door of his stall, and he was presently at large. To his bright mind, of course, the paddle was easy. Out it came, and down poured an avalanche of oats — a bushel, two bushels, and so on to eight or ten. It filled the trough and spilled over to the floor, but Frank was still young and full of ambition, and he buckled down to eat it all.

When Charlie and I found him in the morning he was swelled to the diameter of a wash-tub, his eyes were leaden, and his tongue was hanging out dismally, peppered with oats that he had failed to get down. "The staggers!" exclaimed Charlie, who had become, by that time, an eager but bad amateur horse-doctor. "He is about to bust! There is only one cure. We must run him until it works off." So we squeezed poor Frank between the shafts of the go-cart. leaped in, gave him the whip, and were off. Twice, getting down our hilly road to the pike, he sank to his fore-knees, but both times we got him up, and thereafter, for three hours, we flogged him on. It was a laborious and painful business, and for once in his life Frank failed to laugh at his own joke. Instead, he heaved and panted as if every next breath were to be his last. We could hear his liver and lights rumbling as we forced him on. We were so full of sympathy for him that we quite forgot his burglary, but Charlie insisted that we had to be relentless, and so we were. It was nearing noon when we got back to the stable, and decided to call it a day. Frank drank a bucket of water, stumbled into his stall, and fell headlong in the straw. We let him lie there all afternoon, and all of the night following, and for three days thereafter we kept him on a strict diet of condition powders and Glauber's salt.

The bloating that disfigured him, when it began to go down at last, did not stop at normalcy, but continued until he was as thin as a dying mule, and that thinness persisted for weeks. There came with it, perhaps not unnaturally, a marked distaste for oats. His old voluptuous delight in them was simply gone. He would eat them if nothing else offered, but he never really enjoyed them again. For a year, at least, we might have made him free of a feed-trough full of them without tempting him. What John thought of the episode we could never find out. My guess is that he was too dumb to make anything of it.

III

ADVENTURES OF A

Y.M.C.A. LAD

[*1894*]

WHEN I reach the shades at last it will no doubt astonish Satan to discover, on thumbing my *dossier*, that I was once a member of the Y.M.C.A. Yet a fact is a fact. What is more remarkable, I was not recruited by a missionary to the heathen, but joined at the suggestion of my father, who enjoyed and deserved the name of an infidel. I was then a little beyond fourteen years old, and a new neighborhood branch of the Y, housed in a nobby pressed-brick building, had just been opened in West Baltimore, only a few blocks from our home in Hollins street. The whole upper floor was given over to a gymnasium, and it was this bait, I gathered, that fetched my father, for I was already a bookworm and beginning to be a bit round-shouldered, and he often exhorted me to throw back my shoulders and stick out my chest.

Apparently he was convinced that exercise on the wooden horse and flying rings would cure my scholarly stoop, and make a kind of grenadier of me. If so, he was in error, for I remain more or less Bible-backed to this day, and am often mistaken for a Talmudist. All that the Y.M.C.A.'s horse and rings really accomplished was to fill me with an ineradicable distaste, not only for Christian endeavor in all its forms, but also for every variety of callisthenics, so that I still begrudge the trifling exertion needed to climb in and out of a bathtub, and hate all sports as rabidly as a person who likes sports hates common sense. If I had my way no man guilty of golf would be eligible to any office of trust or profit under the United States, and all female athletes would be shipped to the white-slave corrals of the Argentine.

Indeed, I disliked that gymnasium so earnestly that I never got beyond its baby-class, which was devoted to teaching freshmen how to hang their clothes in the lockers, get into their work-suits, and run round the track. I was in those days a fast runner and could do the 100 yards, with a fair wind, in something better than fourteen seconds, but how anyone could run on a quadrangular track with sides no more than fifty feet long was quite beyond me. The first time I tried it I slipped and slid at all four corners, and the second time I came down with a thump that somehow contrived to skin both my shins. The man in charge of the establishment — the boys all called him Professor — thereupon put me to the punching-bag, but at my fourth or fifth wallop it struck back, and I was floored again. After that I tried all the other insane apparatus in the place, including the horizontal bars, but I always got into trouble very quickly, and never made enough progress to hurt myself seriously, which might have been some comfort, at least on the psychological side. There were other boys who fell from the highest trapezes, and had to be sent home in hacks, and yet others who broke their arms or legs and were heroic figures about the building for months afterward, but the best I ever managed was a bloody nose, and that was caused, not by my own enterprise, but by another boy falling on me from somewhere near the roof. If he had landed six inches farther inshore he might have fractured my skull or broken my neck, but all he achieved was to scrape my nose. It hurt a-plenty, I can tell you, and it hurt still worse when the Professor doused it with arnica, and splashed a couple of drops into each of my eyes.

Looking back over the years, I see that that ghastly gymnasium, if I had continued to frequent it, might have given me an inferiority complex, and bred me up a foe of privilege. I was saved, fortunately, by a congenital complacency that has been a godsend to me, more than once, in other and graver situations. Within a few weeks I was classifying all the boys in the place in the inverse order of their diligence and prowess, and that classification, as I have intimated, I adhere to at the present moment. The youngsters who could leap from bar to bar without slipping and were facile on the trapeze I equated with simians of the genus *Hylobates*, and convinced myself that I was surprised when they showed a capacity for articulate speech. As for the weight-lifters, chinners, somersaulters, leapers and other such virtuosi of striated muscle, I dismissed them as *Anthropoidea* far inferior, in all situations calling for taste or judgment, to schoolteachers or mules.

I should add that my low view of these prizemen was unaccompanied by personal venom; on the contrary, I got on with them very well, and even had a kind of liking for some of them — that is, in their private capacities. Very few, I discovered, were professing Christians, though the Y.M.C.A., in those days even more than now, was a furnace of Protestant divinity. They swore when they stubbed their toes, and the older of them entertained us youngsters in the locker-room with their adventures in amour. The chief free-and-easy trysting-place in West Baltimore, at the time, was a Baptist church specializing in what was called "young people's work." It put on gaudy entertainments, predominantly secular in character, on Sunday nights, and scores of the poor working girls of the section dropped in to help with the singing and lasso beaux. I gathered from the locker-room talk that some of those beaux demanded dreadful prices for their consent to the lassoing. Whether this boasting was true or not I did not know, for I never attended the Sabbath evening orgies myself, but at all events it showed that those who did so were of an antinomian tendency, and far from ideal Y.M.C.A. fodder. When the secretaries came to the gymnasium to drum up customers for prayer-meetings downstairs the Lotharios always sounded razzberries and cleared out.

On one point all hands were agreed, and that was on the point that the Professor was what, in those days, was called a pain in the neck. When he mounted a bench and yelled "Fellows!" my own blood always ran cold, and his subsequent remarks gave me a touch of homicidal mania. Not until many years afterward, when a certain eminent politician in Washington took to radio crooning, did I ever hear a more offensive voice. There were tones in it like the sound of molasses dripping from a barrel. It was not at all effeminate, but simply saccharine. Had I been older in worldly wisdom it would have suggested to me a suburban curate gargling over the carcass of a usurer who had just left the parish its richest and stupidest widow. As I was, an innocent boy, I could only compare it to the official chirping of a Sunday-school superintendent. What the Professor had to say was usually sensible enough, and I don't recall him ever mentioning either Heaven or Hell; it was simply his tone and manner that offended me. He is now dead, I take it, for many years, and I only hope that he has had good luck *post mortem*, but while he lived his harangues to his students gave me a great deal of unnecessary pain, and definitely slanted my mind against the Y.M.C.A. Even when, many years later, I discovered as a newspaper correspondent that the Berlin outpost thereof, under the name of the *christliche Verein junger Männer*, was so enlightened that it served beer in its lamissary, I declined to change my attitude.

But I was driven out of the Y.M.C.A. at last, not by the Professor nor even by his pupils in the odoriferous gymnasium — what a foul smell, indeed, a gymnasium has! how it suggests a mixture of Salvation Army, elephant house, and county jail! — but by a young member who, so far as I observed, never entered the Professor's domain at all. He was a pimply, officious fellow of seventeen or eighteen, and to me, of course, he seemed virtually a grown man. The scene of his operations was the reading-room, whither I often resorted in self-defense when the Professor let go with "Fellows!" and began one of his hortations. It was quiet there, and though most of the literature on tap was pietistic I enjoyed going through it, for my long interest in the sacred sciences had already begun. One evening, while engaged upon a pamphlet detailing devices for catching boys and girls who knocked down part of their Sunday-school money, I became aware of the pimply one, and presently saw him go to a bookcase and select a book. Dropping into a chair, he turned its pages feverishly, and presently he found what he seemed to be looking for, and cleared his throat to attract attention. The four or five of us at the long table all looked up.

"See here, fellows," he began — again that ghastly "fellows!" — "let me have your ears for just a moment. Here is a book" — holding it up — "that is worth all the other books ever written by mortal man. There is nothing like it on earth except the One Book that our Heavenly Father Himself gave us. It is pure gold, pure meat. There is not a wasted word in it. Every syllable is a perfect gem. For example, listen to this —"

What it was he read I don't recall precisely, but I remember that it was some thumping and appalling platitude or other — something on the order of "Honesty is the best policy," "A guilty conscience needs no accuser," or "It is never too late to mend." I guessed at first that he was trying to be ironical, but it quickly appeared that he was quite serious, and before his audience managed to escape he had read forty or fifty such specimens of otiose rubbish, and following nearly every one of them he indulged himself in a little homily, pointing up its loveliness and rubbing in its lesson. The poor ass, it appeared, was actually enchanted, and wanted to spread his joy. It was easy to recognize in him the anti-social animus of a born evangelist, but there was also something else — a kind of voluptuous delight in the shabby and preposterous, a perverted aestheticism like that of a latter-day movie or radio fan, a wild will to roll in and snuffle balderdash as a cat rolls in and snuffles catnip. I was, as I have said, less than fifteen years old, but I had already got an overdose of such blah in the McGuffey Readers and penmanship copybooks of the time, so I withdrew as quickly as possible, unhappily aware that even the Professor was easier to take than this jitney Dwight L. Moody. I got home all tuckered out, and told my father (who was sitting up reading for the tenth or twentieth time a newspaper account of the hanging of two labor leaders) that the Y.M.C.A. fell a good deal short of what it was cracked up to be.

He bade me go back the next evening and try again, and I did so in filial duty. Indeed, I did so a dozen or more nights running, omitting Sundays, when the place was given over to spiritual exercises exclusively. But each and every night that imbecile was in the reading-room, and each and every night he read from that revolting book to all within ear-shot. I gathered gradually that it was having a great run in devotional circles, and was, in fact, a sort of moral best-seller. The author, it appeared, was a Methodist bishop, and a great hand at inculcating righteousness. He not only knew by heart all the immemorial platitudes, stretching back to the days of Gog and Magog; he had also invented many more or less new ones, and it was these novelties that especially aroused the enthusiasm of his disciple. I wish I could recall some of them, but my memory has always had a humane faculty for obliterating the intolerable, and so I can't. But you may take my word for it that nothing in the subsequent writings of Dr. Orison Swett Marden or Dr. Frank Crane was worse.

In a little while my deliverance was at hand, for though my father had shown only irritation when I described to him the pulpit manner of the Professor, he was immediately sympathetic when I told him about the bishop's book, and the papuliferous exegete's laboring of it. " You had better quit," he said, " before you hit him with a spittoon, or go crazy. There ought to be a law against such roosters." *Rooster* was then his counter-word, and might signify anything from the most high-toned and elegant Shriner, bank cashier or bartender to the most scurvy and abandoned Socialist. This time he used it in its most opprobrious sense, and so my career in the Y.M.C.A. came to an end. I carried away from it, not only an indelible distrust of every sort of athlete, but also a loathing of Methodist bishops, and it was many years afterward before I could bring myself to admit any such right rev. father in God to my friendship. I have since learned that some of them are very pleasant and amusing fellows, despite their professional enmity to the human race, but the one who wrote that book was certainly nothing of the sort. If, at his decease, he escaped Hell, then moral theology is as full of false alarms as secular law.

IV

THE EDUCATIONAL PROCESS

[*1896*]

Why my father sent me to the Baltimore Polytechnic I have never been able to make out, though from time to time I have fetched up various more or less colorable theories — and seen them go to pot when confronted with the known facts. I had, as a boy, the usual boyish interest in making things, but I soon discovered that I had no talent for it, and so my interest gradually died down. My mother was full of stories of my striking incapacity for the constructive chores of the household; indeed, she depicted me as only a little less incompetent than my father, who could not mount a ladder without falling off or drive a nail without mashing his thumb. One Summer, when we were at our country place, she gave me the job of making a table for a storeroom and I fell to work reluctantly but violently, using a pile of old joists and flooring as materials. When the thing was done it was so massive and clumsy that I could not move it into the corner where it was to stand, and the hired girl had to be called in to help. It stood in that corner until the house was sold after my father's death, and I heard later from the buyer that he had a dreadful time getting rid of it. Since it would not go through either of the doors of the room, it had to be knocked to pieces on the spot, and this turned out to be a laborious job, for I had put it together with fifty-penny iron nails running fourteen to the pound, and had not been stingy with them. These nails had rusted, and the only way to get them out was to split the wood, which was anything but easy, for the joists were of yellow pine of irregular grain and very knotty. By the time the buyer poured this tale into my ear I had passed through the Polytechnic and held its diploma, but if I had been put to making another such table I'd have made it just as badly, for I don't recall learning anything of a mechanical nature while I was a student. I enjoyed some of the shop work, especially the wood-turning and blacksmithing, but that was mainly because it was a rather hazardous kind of play; it left no more sediment of profit in my mind than the prayers the president of the school used to let go in the assembly-room every morning.

My actual interests, in those days, lay far from tools and machinery. I was fascinated, on the one hand, by the art of writing and on the other by the science of chemistry, and both obsessions had been set going by Christmas presents — the first by that of a printing-press and the second by that of a camera. The two fought it out in my psyche all the while I was in the Polytechnic, and it was only in my last year that the writing insanity won. My first effort to write for publication was a sort of compromise between them, for it took the form of a report on a platinum solution that I had devised for toning silver prints. This was during the Summer of 1894, when I was still less than fourteen years old. Writing won in the end largely if not principally because the brethren who expounded *literae humaniores* at the Polytechnic were both enthusiasts, whereas the brother who taught chemistry knew very little about it and appeared to have only mild interest in it. Of the former, there were two, and both of them, by the ordinary academic standards of the time, were bad teachers. Moreover, they failed as moral exemplars, for one chewed tobacco incessantly and the other often showed up in class of a morning with bleary eyes and a breath like a sailor home from the sea. But they had in common an ardent and almost pious delight in good writing, and in their catch-as-catch-can way they managed somehow to convey it to such of the boys as were susceptible to such infections. Neither taught composition *qua* composition, but they knew where the best models of it were to be found, and I recall brilliantly over all these years what delights shot through me when one of them set me to reading the *Spectator* and the other introduced me to Thackeray. No other gogues in the place matched them in fanning my private fires, so I got more out of them than from all the rest, and what I got was better lasting. Between them they converted me into one of the most assiduous customers that the Enoch Pratt Free Library in Baltimore has had in its whole history. There were Winters when I visited it almost every week-day, and before I began to be fetched by the literary movement of the nineties I had read at least half of the classical English répertoire.

But I don't want to say that the other gogues at the Polytechnic were all hams, for some of them were clearly not, especially two teachers of mathematics, a subject in which I had little interest. To one of these obscure Bernoullis I owe a massive debt, and it is a pleasant privilege to acknowledge it gratefully after fifty years. He was a man named Uhrbrock, an eccentric bachelor of unknown provenance and training, and his learning in his chosen art probably went but little beyond the algebra that he taught. But he had the great merit of believing in all seriousness that algebra was a discipline of stupendous importance to civilization, and in consequence he imparted it with a degree of zeal amounting almost to frenzy. When I proceeded to the Polytechnic from F. Knapp's Institute in 1892, I was quite innocent of it, for old Professor Knapp had different ideas, and the idiot gogues who sorted out incoming boys thus put me in the lowest class. In all other respects I was ready to enter the next higher class, but the idiots stuck to the letter of their rules. In some way or other Uhrbrock heard of this, and at once offered to tutor me privately — that is, if I were willing to stay an hour after school every day until he judged that I knew enough to be promoted. I was willing, and he fell on me in his most furious manner. For a few days my head swam, but after that I began to take in algebra by the eye, the ear and the pores of my skin, and by the middle of the second week I knew everything that the boys were supposed to learn that first year. Uhrbrock thereupon took me before the committee of idiots, demanded that I be examined, stood by menacingly while they questioned me, and terrorized them into passing me with a mark of 100. The next day I was promoted, and ever since that time, down to the present glorious day, I have been a year ahead of schedule on my progress through life. I say this because, on age alone, I really belonged in the lowest class. But Professor Knapp and his goons had done such a good job of teaching me all the branches save algebra that I had almost accumulated the extra year, and it needed only Uhrbrock's philanthropy to give it to me.

I call it philanthropy advisedly, though in general philanthropy seems to me to be a purely imaginary quantity, like demi-virginity or one glass of beer. Even here, I suppose, I am forgetting the lust to teach — a passion apparently analogous to concupiscence or dipsomania, and, in the more extreme varieties of pedagogues, maybe quite as strong. I daresay that Uhrbrock was full of it, but I must point out in fairness that his yielding to it went a good deal further than has ever been usual in his order. If he merely lusted to teach he might have worked out his libido within the ordinary patterns of the place; as it was, he stepped outside them, and put himself to purely gratuitous trouble. If I had to stay after school every day, in hot September weather, then so did he. Moreover, his willingness to do this for a perfect stranger certainly had some sort of altruism in it, at least to the extent that you will find altruism in the operations of the F.B.I. or the Boy Scouts. He had never seen or heard of me before, and in fact had to ask my name ten or twenty times before he remembered it. Nor was I the bright and shining sort of youngster who may be expected to attract adult notice and favor; on the contrary, I was more unprepossessing than otherwise, with a bulging cranium, round shoulders, bow legs, and very little show of the prancing masculine gorgeousness that developed later. Thus I was very grateful to Uhrbrock for what he did for me, and shall go on thinking of it as philanthropy. In the years following, I should add in candor, he made some efforts to cash in on it. I was by that time the city editor of a newspaper in Baltimore, and he was involved in a row with his superiors — a row that went on for a long, long while. Whenever it rose to special venom he would visit me at my office and try to induce me to print his diatribes against his opponents. Inasmuch as those diatribes had but slight support in any facts known to me and many of them were packed with libel *per se*, I had to put him off, but I was always very polite to him, and whenever the chance offered to give him a little sneaking aid I seized it. In the end his enemies got him and he was drummed out of the public school system, and soon afterward he died.

He was a competent teacher, and rammed the mysteries of algebra into his boys with great success. Some of them actually became so proficient that they could solve the problems he set to them without any sort of cheating. His colleagues of the mathematical faculty were generally less proficient, and it was therefore the custom of the school to use cribs against them. One of these colleagues, an old fellow who had been a pedagogue for many years, and showed all the traditional stigmata of the craft — a pasty complexion, chalky fingers, and a preference for white neckties and black alpaca coats — eventually gave great delight to his pupils by going crazy. His infirmity crept upon him slowly, and in its earlier stages all that was noticed was that he was more crabbed than usual. When a boy went to the blackboard to solve a problem in geometry or trigonometry he would fall upon the poor fellow like a cat playing a mouse, and try to rattle him with frequent cries of "Nonsense!", always pronounced with the two syllables equally stressed. Nine times out of ten the boy had a copy of the solution in his hand, lifted from the textbook, and had simply transferred it to the board, but the old man nevertheless found plenty to object to. In the end he began to question and deride the book itself, and it dawned upon the boys that he had gone *mashuggah*. Proof positive followed almost instantly, for he took to felicitating and whooping up the occasional boys who were too stupid to use the book solutions, or maybe even too honest. In a little while some smartie tried him out with a solution so fantastically imbecile that the dullest boys laughed at it. When he praised it as a masterpiece everyone knew for sure that his mind had happily given way, and thereafter all of his students were magnificently at ease in his classroom. My own class, which visited him twice a week, had a rollicking time. The more fatuous the solution offered, the better he liked it, so we gave him what he wanted, and got high marks day after day. Now and then, to test the progress of his malady, we put up controls armed with cribs from the textbook. Each and every time he drove them from the blackboard with yells of " Nonsense! " and we thus established the fact that he was not recovering. The boys of all his classes naturally kept his lunacy to themselves, and it was weeks before any of the other gogues noticed it. The poor old fellow was then relieved of his duties, and his successor gave us a really savage working out. At the end of that year more than half the boys in my class were plucked in mathematics, but the administration let them go on the ground that we had all suffered through no fault of our own. No boy, of course, was conscious of any actual suffering.

This unhappy gogue was a pretty good teacher in his days of normalcy, though not as good as Uhrbrock. Most of the other members of the faculty, with the shining exception of the two who professed English literature, ranged downward from indifferent to unspeakable. The great sciences of anatomy and physiology, naturally extremely interesting to adolescent boys, were in charge of a superannuated homeopath armed with a textbook in which all the abdomen south of the umbilicus was represented by a smooth and quite uneventful surface, exactly like the figleaf section of a female acrobat's pink tights. The homeopath, who must have gone through some sort of medical college in his time, was apparently convinced that he could never arouse any interest in his subject with such reticent materials, for he made no effort whatsoever to teach it. Instead, he devoted his lecture periods to rambling harangues on all sorts of non-anatomical subjects, and every boy knew that all who listened with any show of attention would get high passing marks at the end of the year. His principal business was really not teaching at all, but the coopering of boys injured in the shops. This happened very frequently, and he seldom got through one of his harangues without having to stop to sew up a cut or pull out a splinter. His assembled students always watched these manipulations with fascination, and some of them, called on for occasional help, became skillful operating-room orderlies. It was not often that a boy was hurt seriously, but once it happened in my presence. The victim was a handsome young fellow who was so well liked that he had been made president of my class. Like all the rest of us, he had been warned against the extreme dangers of using a power plane to dress thin pieces of wood, but one day he chose to disregard them, his piece of wood gave way, the fingers of his right hand were sucked into the revolving blades, and he lost every finger save the thumb. I was standing not six feet away from him, and the bloody spectacle shocked me even more than it did the victim, who bore it very bravely. We did not take him to the homeopath, but rushed him to the City Hospital, which was separated from the Polytechnic only by an alley. There the surgical interns stopped the hemorrhage and sewed up the stumps, but his fingers were gone forever — a cruel calamity to an ambitious youngster.

One of the boys retrieved them from the pile of shavings under the plane, and brought them to the hospital, hoping that they could be sewed on, but the interns said that in the then state of surgery it could not be done.

There was a medical school attached to the hospital, and its students loafed and skylarked in the alley separating them from the Polytechnic. We were on friendly terms with them, and they entertained us by showing off their horrors. Also, they were of assistance to us in our wars with unpopular teachers. After we had bombarded one such unfortunate with all the classical weapons, including live rats and hydrogen sulphide, the medical students gave us an ear from an Aframerican cadaver, and we stuffed it into his inkwell. But this *attentat*, despite its boldness and ingenuity, was a failure, for the gogue, a very stupid fellow, fished the ear out of his ink and dropped it into his wastebasket without a word, and we spent the next week trying to figure out whether he had really recognized it for what it was. There was a faction that proposed to give him another and surer shock by getting a whole Aframerican head from the medical students and propping it up on his desk, but the students refused to supply it. The disappearance of an ear, they said, would pass unnoticed, but if they made off with a head there would be an inquiry and maybe a good deal of unpleasantness. Some years after this it was discovered that the *Diener* in the dissecting-room of the college had been carrying on for years a brisk trade in entire cadavers. He filched them from the morgue in the basement, crammed them into barrels, and shipped them to fly-by-night medical colleges in the West. By the time he was taken I was already out of the Polytechnic and working as a newspaper reporter, and it fell to me to cover the story of his arrest, trial and jugging.

The shop-work at the Polytechnic, as I have said, interested me very little, save for that in the wood-turning and blacksmith shops. For some reason or other I got pleasure out of making the puerile gimcracks that were the chief product of the former, and there was always the stimulating possibility that one of the pointed tools we used would dig into the wood — we called it catching a crab — and make a kind of explosion. Such accidents always brought the gogue in charge of the shop at a run, and he would stop all work and deliver himself of a long monitory lecture. He was an old fellow in a skullcap that made him look like a rabbi and his lectures were heavy going. We took his warnings lightly, but once I saw a block of maple, caught in a crab, fly from the lathe with such force that when it hit the guilty boy in the forehead he went out like a pug caught in the jaw. By the time he revived and we took him to the homeopath he had a bump on his forehead as big as an egg. Another time, in the same shop, a power-operated bandsaw broke, and the boy using it was wound up in the blade. His injuries, however, consisted only of a few minor cuts, and the homeopath soon had him patched up and on his way home. I liked the blacksmith shop because it was full of sparks and noise, and also, I suppose, because it was dirty. In it, after four or five months of hard struggle, I made a small iron hook that I still use as a paperweight. In it I also received the only injury I suffered in four years at the Polytechnic. It was, naturally enough, a burn, and I got it by picking up a piece of iron that looked cold to the eye but was actually still very hot. Having got hold of it, I couldn't let go, and in consequence my hand was burned badly enough to give me three or four days' holiday. I often worked in the chemical laboratory after school hours, but was never hurt there, though I had several narrow escapes. One day a boy working next to me filled a test-tube with nitric acid, plugged it with a cork, and proceeded in all innocence to heat it over a Bunsen burner. When it went off I managed to duck the murderous spatter, but the boy responsible got a big splash down one of his bare arms, and before I could douse him with an alkali a sizable groove was burned into his flesh.

It was the custom at the school for the boys of the senior class to make an ambitious piece of machinery, and my class undertook a 100-horsepower triple-expansion marine engine. The plans came from the Naval Academy at Annapolis and the castings were made outside, but we did all the machining. I say we, but my own share was confined to finishing the crosshead brasses, for my talents were too modest for me to be entrusted with anything more vital. I worked on those brasses all year, and ruined two or three sets of castings before I produced a finished set that fit. The best machinist in my class, a really competent fellow, got the lordly job of boring the cylinders, and was a hero in consequence. He and the instructor, who knew his subject as few other teachers in the place knew theirs, spent a lot of time counselling and helping me, but my congenital incapacity for mechanical operations kept me in the baby class. My diligence, however, got its reward, for at the end of the year, though I must have been a headache to him, the instructor gave me a good mark.

The president of the Polytechnic, in those remote days, was a retired naval lieutenant — a tall, slim, elegant fellow wearing the mustache and goatee of Admiral Winfield Scott Schley, then a common make-up among naval officers. He was supposed to teach us the higher arcana of steam engineering, but he was so bad a teacher that we had to get whatever we actually learned of the subject from the instructor in the machine-shop. I well recall my difficulties in trying to puzzle out the mysteries of an indicator diagram — a sort of chart showing the performance of a steam-engine. After listening to the lieutenant for a month or two I gave it up as hopeless, but a little while later the machine-shop instructor made it plain to me in ten minutes. I forgot it, of course, within twenty-four hours after the Polytechnic's diploma was in my hands, as I forgot virtually everything else that I had, at least in theory, learned there. At the present moment I am probably as far from a mechanical genius as it is possible for the free white American to get, and still maintain any degree of public veneration. A gasoline engine is as completely mysterious to me as the way of a serpent upon a rock, and when a fuse blows out in my house and I have to replace it the job takes me the better part of an hour.

The naval lieutenant had the easy ways of a sailor and was very popular with the boys. When they started an insurrection in the room of some numskull gogue he would let them roar on for five or ten minutes before coming in to put it down. Such events were commonly followed by mass trials, with himself as judge, but he seldom found anyone guilty and when he did so his punishments were so trivial as to be almost rewards. He had, like any other man of service on the high seas, an eye for female pulchritude, and was known to receive visits from the fair in his office after school hours. Inasmuch as the boys who observed this always reported that his visitors were beauties on the order of the loveliest actresses portrayed on the cigarette-cards of the time, the news only increased his popularity. But not with the gogues who were his subordinates. They were, in the main, creatures so unattractive to either sex that it would be impossible to imagine even Lydia Pinkham calling on them, so they viewed his gallantries with bilious eyes, and in the end one of them laid charges against him with the school board. Those charges, as reported in the newspapers, were rather vague, but it was easy to gather that they accused the old boy of levantine carnalities. By the time they came out I had left the Polytechnic, but I was interested enough to inquire how the surviving boys had taken the business, and got an answer that pleased me greatly. The day after the outcry, as the lieutenant entered the assembly-room to lead in morning prayers, the whole student body rose as one boy and launched into such a riot of cheers that the cop on the beat came rushing in. A little later, apparently fearing that the names of definite ladies might be brought into the case, he resigned without standing trial, and on his departure got another deafening round of huzzahs. He was succeeded by another naval lieutenant, and this one, after a while, was also beset by the school wowsers. They charged him with resorting to the jug during school hours, and he demanded and received a public trial. Acquitted triumphantly, he got a reception from the boys almost but not quite equalling the deafening approbation of his predecessor. The latter remains to this day the greatest hero the Baltimore Polytechnic has ever produced. The boys, I am told, still cheer him at football games, though they were not born at the time of his troubles, and many of them are the sons of men who were not then born.

If I had encountered a good teacher of chemistry at the Polytechnic, it is very probable that I'd be a chemist at this moment, with a swell job on the staff of the du Ponts and maybe a couple of new synthetic rubbers or super-cellophanes to my credit. My chief interest was always in organic chemistry, but the best that was offered by the gogue aforesaid was a childish high-school course in inorganic analysis, so I began, in a kind of despair, to work off my steam in literary endeavor. My early compositions, of course, were mainly in verse, for poetry is much easier to write than prose. During my last year in school I turned out many a fair set of dithyrambs, most of them in imitation of Rudyard Kipling, who had become my adoration, and the rest in the old French forms that were favored by the literary movement of the nineties. I recall that at one time, probably during my last year at the Polytechnic, I resolved solemnly to write at least one poem a day, and that I kept it up for several weeks. But it was more than a year after my graduation before anything of mine ever got into print. During my school days I nursed a flaming ambition to be admitted to the staff of the school paper, but I kept it to myself, and was never asked to join by the politicoes who bossed such things. As a sort of final blast at the gogues the boys of my class concocted a satirical musical comedy, but though I wrote a couple of lyrics for it I had no hand in the prose scurrilities which made it a great success, and at the one performance I was told off to play the piano. Some of the more tender gogues were so outraged by the sneers at them that they talked boldly of holding up several diplomas, but the old lieutenant with the stable of lovely sweeties was still president, and he put down his heavy quarter-deck foot upon the project.

I made a pretty good scholastic record during my four years at the Polytechnic, despite my lack of interest in most of the subjects it presumed to teach. In the literary branches I really shined, and I found mathematics easy, though I disliked it. At the end of my term of servitude there was a general examination for the purpose of awarding a gold medal offered by the Alumni Association to the master scholar of the whole herd. This award was made on the basis of the examination alone, and classroom marks were not taken into account. The first day was devoted to English, and I was passed at the head of my class. The next day there was an examination in something else that happened to be easy for me, and I passed first again. When I got home with this news my father went into a state of mystical exaltation, and then stepped out of it with an offer to give me $100 in cash if I remained in first place at the end of the examinations. This seemed a hard order, for there were subjects ahead — for example, electricity — of which I knew precisely nothing, but a hundred dollars, in those days, was a fabulous fortune to a boy, and I resolved to make the attempt. My experience with Uhrbrock, four years before, had taught me something, to wit, that with hard application a subject that engaged a class a whole year could be wolfed in a few days. Favored by the fact that there was a free day between adjoining examinations, I gave it over to relentless boning up on the subject just ahead, and the result was, to make a long and painful story short, that I passed all the examinations and came out at the head of my class; indeed, I came out with a general average that has not been surpassed at the Polytechnic, so far as I know, to this day. Fortune, of course, gave me a good deal of assistance, for I was born lucky. When I came, for example, to the examination in electricity I discovered to my enchantment that the twelve questions on the paper all covered ground that I had traversed the night before, my nose in the book and the midnight oil burning. In consequence, my answers were perfect, and the amazed and disgusted gogue in charge of the examination had to give me a mark of 100. In addition to the alumni medal there was a special medal for the ranking scholar in electricity — and I had won it!

But giving it to me was something else again. The poor gogue, justifiably horrified, came out the next day with an announcement that monthly marks would be taken into account in awarding the medal, which would hand it over to a boy who really knew something about the subject. This seemed to me to be reasonable and fair, and I was glad to see him get it, but my father professed to be outraged and talked wildly of going into court for an injunction against the school board. It took me some time to argue him out of this, but in the end he calmed down, and when I brought him the news that I was to be allowed to make a speech at the commencement he forgot the matter. That speech must have been a dreadful thing, indeed, for I was still very young in those days, and had not yet acquired my present facility for rabble-rousing. But my father listened to it very politely, and he and his agents applauded it loudly when it was over. I was myself too elevated to be conscious of its badness, for his check for $100 was in the inside pocket of my tail-coat. It was not until I was approaching twenty-five that I ever earned $100 in one lump again.

V

FINALE

TO THE ROGUE'S MARCH

[*1900*]

WHEN I was disgorged by the Polytechnic I went to work in my father's cigar factory, theoretically to learn the tobacco business, but *Geschäft* was not to my taste, and when my father died in 1899 I quit at once and got myself a job as a cub reporter on the old Baltimore *Morning Herald*, now extinct and almost forgotten. At the start, of course, I was not entrusted with news stories of any importance, but simply served as a leg man for my elders and betters. One of the first big stories I thus helped to cover was the hanging of four blackamoors at the Baltimore City Jail. It was worth, by the standards of the time, two or three columns of space, so the reporter assigned to it was a fellow of some esteem in the office, despite an unhappy weakness for drink.

As for me, I had no responsibility beyond getting the correct spelling of the attending ecclesiastics' names, taking down the last words (if any) of the condemned, and inquiring into the undertaking arrangements. But that programme was quickly blown up by the fact of my senior's addiction to the so-called hand-set whiskey of the Baltimore printers, which kept him sound asleep in the warden's office all the while the hanging was going on, got him fired when we returned to our own office, and set me to writing the story. The taste of the period, in all such branches of composition, was for prose so colorful as to be virtually purple, and I must have laid on my pigments with a shovel, for the city editor gave me a very kind look when the proofs came down, and I had first call on every similar assignment afterward.

I found the work light and instructive, and there was plenty of it to do, for a movement was afoot in my native Maryland at the time to "hang out," as the phrase went, the whole criminal population of the state, at all events in the higher brackets. The notion that murderers, rapists and other such fiends in human form were simply unfortunates suffering from mental croups and catarrhs, and that the sensible way to deal with them was to send them to luxurious sanatoria, and there ply them with nourishing victuals, moral suasion and personality tests — that notion was still hidden in the womb of the future. The prevailing therapy was a great deal harsher: in fact, it came down from the rough-and-ready days of Leviticus and Deuteronomy, and its only recent improvements had been developed during the California gold rush. It consisted, in brief, in pursuing the erring with cops, posses and bloodhounds, putting them on trial before hanging judges, and then dispatching them as promptly as possible. As a young reporter I observed and recorded all branches of this *régimen,* and enjoyed them all. But I enjoyed especially the terminal part, for my lifelong interest in theology was already well developed, and it gave me a great kick to hobnob and palaver with the divines who comforted the doomed.

These divines, of course, were mainly Aframericans, for the great majority of culprits hanged below the Mason and Dixon Line were of that great race, but though it is usually thought of down there as somewhat backward I never saw any sign of professional incompetence in its pastors. On the contrary, they were almost invariably smart and snappy fellows, well grounded in the Sacred Scriptures and the masters of an adroit and effective homiletic technic. The job they had on their hands, in the normal case, was certainly no easy one. What they had to do was to convince a blackamoor taken red-handed in some brutal and deliberate atrocity, usually freely admitted, that he would nevertheless get a free pardon for it post-mortem, and in fact become an angel in Heaven, white in color and of the highest repute, within ten minutes of his exitus from this earth. There were, to be sure, parts of this that needed no arguing, for they were not disputed. Every colored brother in the death-house, like every colored person of his class outside, believed in Heaven and Hell, looked forward to a drum-head trial for his sins after death, and had an unshakable faith that, in case of acquittal, he would be turned into a Caucasian angel. But that was only the half of it, and what remained must have been a great deal harder to inculcate, for it collided with everything that the candidate had been taught by other clergymen his whole life long. One and all they had concentrated on the pains and penalties of Hell, and had warned him *appassionata* and *con amore* that he would be inevitably fried in its fires if he did not curb his evil propensities. But now, having yielded the last measure of devotion to those propensities, he was asked to believe that he would escape Hell altogether, and even meet with what amounted to special handling in Heaven.

It seeemd irrational, surely, and not a few of the colored boys wrestled with it dismally for weeks and months. If things would actually be so facile and comfortable beyond the grave, then why all the horrible talk about the boiling sulphur and steaming geysers of Hell? And if Hell was a myth, then why ever be good at all, even in intent? Such were the questions the death-house divines had to answer, and how they answered them I can't tell you with any definiteness, though I often listened to their explanations for hours. They must have been experts at suggestion and virtuosi at untangling complexes, though both suggestion and complexes were unheard of at the time. All I can say is that, when the job was done at last, the client still retained his full faith in Hell, along with the utmost confidence in its system of justice, and yet was completely convinced that he would escape its fires. In his terminal days, in fact, he usually gloated openly over his approaching apotheosis, and not infrequently showed a certain smugness. Let the sheriff do his damndest: he might hang a poor coon, but out of that coon, like a butterfly from a caterpillar, would emerge a celestial creature with large, snowy wings and a complexion to match that of any white lady in the land, however rich and beautiful.

Such ideas naturally take away the sting of death, and it was not uncommon for the postulants to go to the gallows as jauntily as if they were going to a barber shop. I saw some who actually pranced — that is, to the extent that it was possible in their long black gowns, and with their arms tied behind them. When they had anything to say in their last minutes, which was usually, it was always of an extremely optimistic nature, and whenever they mentioned individuals by name — say the sheriff, the warden, the pastor, or a guard of the death-watch — it was in terms of praise. I recall one — it was on the Eastern Shore of Maryland — who devoted most of his farewell remarks to whooping up the jail cook, for the whole time since his trial had been eased by fried chicken and hominy cakes three times a day. Another even had a kind word for the Governor who had refused to reprieve him, and expressed regret that his approaching translation would make it impossible for him to vote at the coming election, in which the Governor would be running for a second term. But mostly, of course, they talked of themselves, for the glories that awaited them naturally engrossed them. I have never heard more eloquent descriptions of the geography, social life and public improvements of Heaven than some of those that were thus loosed by uneducated but not untutored Aframericans upon audiences of newspaper reporters, professional jurymen, country constables and courthouse loafers.

There was, however, one exception to the general rule I have set forth, and him I encountered in the city jail of Baltimore — an ancient granite structure in the feudal style of architecture, with crenellated battlements along the tops of its walls, and accommodation in its death-house, in those days, for a dozen head of condemned. It was a gloomy place, God knows, and not all the colored theologians of Baltimore, working in eight-hour shifts for weeks on end, could lift its darkness for the unhappy blackamoor I speak of. For he had been, in his time, a preacher himself, and though he had later turned apostate and was now awaiting hanging for murdering a whole family, he still retained his old talent for the sacred sciences, and especially for theological disputation. Thus he sassed back when the death-house clergy began to operate on him, and in a little while he had them completely flabbergasted. Unhappily, his success against them was his undoing, for he retained, like any other sane colored man, his full belief in Hell, and the more he proved that their talk of his becoming an angel was hooey, the more he convinced himself (and them) that he was headed for the brimstone. This naturally upset him considerably, and as the day of his departure approached he became more and more alarmed. On the morning thereof he was in a really appalling state. All he had to do, if he wanted to see a swarm of devils with their pitchforks, was to shut his eyes. Even his appetite left him, and he actually refused the magnificent breakfast that was brought to him. He was to be hanged, if the sheriff was not diverted by some other duty, at 10 a.m., and by 9.45 he was making such heavy weather of it that the jail doctor, a very humane man, decided to give him a shot of morphine.

I was present when this shot went into his arm, and noted the dose — three grains. Inasmuch as a quarter of a grain is ordinarily enough to quiet a patient, and two grains enough to quiet him forever, it was apparent that the doctor was taking no chances. He watched with satisfaction, and I watched with him, the rapidly gathering effects of the drug. First the candidate ceased to moan and bellow, then his speech became thick, then his eyes began to roll, then he sat down on his bed, and then he looked at us blankly, apparently not recognizing us. The minutes, meanwhile, were ticking on, and the doctor himself grew uneasy. In fifteen more of them his patient would be blotto, and hanging him might present serious technical difficulties. Where was the sheriff? Why the delay? Just then a deputy came galloping from the warden's office with the news that the sheriff was on the telephone — an arduous business in those days —, trying to track down a rumor that the Governor had decided to grant the condemned a five-days' reprieve.

The doctor lost no time. He was in the warden's office in ten seconds, and back with the sheriff in half a minute. "Either you hang this coon at once," he roared, "or he'll die in your face! He has got enough morphine aboard to knock off an archbishop. Look at him! He doesn't know whether he is here or in Indianapolis, Indiana. In an hour he'll be dead. Get a hump on! Get a hump on! You were supposed to hang him at ten o'clock, and it's now ten six. Do you want to go to jail for contempt of court? Get a hump on! Get a hump on!"

The sheriff, in a panic, got it on instanter, and in two minutes the condemned was being half led and half carried down the corridor, his eyes rolling more and more and his head beginning to roll too. There was some difficulty about getting him up the steps of the scaffold, but a dozen jail guards leaped forward to help, and at ten o'clock, sixteen minutes and twenty seconds a.m. he went through the trap. His eyes were closed in his last moments and his knees were buckling, but not from fear. He had forgotten all about the Christian Heaven and Hell, and was neck-deep in the poppy Paradise of the Chinese.

After a colored undertaker had made off with the remains the sheriff finally got the Governor's office by telephone, and learned that the report of a reprieve had been a canard. The next day, encountering the jail doctor in a saloon, I asked him what he would have done if it had turned out to be true.

"I'd have made out a death-certificate," he replied calmly, blowing the foam off a schooner, "saying that he died of fright."

"But," I persisted, "you couldn't have signed it. You know the law: it provides that there must be a coroner's inquest after every death in jail, and that the coroner must sign the death-certificate."

"As for that," he replied, still calm, "the coroner and I have an understanding. We always cooperate professionally."

VI

NOTES

ON PALAEOZOIC PUBLICISTS

[*1902*]

IT is the fashion today, in newspaper circles, to sniff at press-agents, and even to spit at them: in the *Editor and Publisher*, the trade journal of the daily press, they are treated as if they were lepers, or even infidels. That was certainly not my own feeling about them in the days when I had most to do with them, *circa* 1902. I had by then become what was called the dramatic editor of the *Morning Herald* in Baltimore, and one of my jobs was to receive the press-agents who traveled ahead of itinerant theatrical troupes, whooping up the genius of their stars. Nine-tenths of these brethren seemed to me to be very pleasant fellows, and some of them were so smart that they afterward made considerable splashes in the world, whether inside the bounds of the theatre or out — for example, Eugene Walter, Channing Pollock, the Wilstach brothers, Charles Emerson Cook, Bayard Veiller and Herbert Bayard Swope. Nearly all had been newspaper men in their time, and good ones. I cannot say that I was very generous about giving them space; on the contrary, I held them down to short commons, and often spoiled the little matter I printed by adding clownish glosses to it; nevertheless, I got on with them very well, and made some friendships among them that endure to this day.

In that remote era some of the primeval press-agents of the post-Civil War period still survived, and still wore the long-tailed coats, loud waistcoats and plug hats that had then gone with their art and mystery. The first agent who ever called on me, in fact, was of that already archaic company. He was at least sixty years old, and looked to me to be a hundred. His talk was all about Lotta, Maggie Mitchell, Charlotte Cushman, Mary Anderson and other such old-timers, though he was actually working for a young female star who, according to his story, had but lately escaped from a convent in Mauch Chunk, Pa. All his purple prose about her was done with a lead-pencil on large sheets of ruled yellow paper, for he regarded the typewriter as effeminate. Another elderly visitor who made a great impression on me was a splendid creature of the name of Marcus B. Mayer. He had been an opera manager in his day, and had carried over into press-agentry the uniform of that calling — a fur overcoat, a white waistcoat elegantly embroidered, and a gold-headed walking stick. What star he represented I forget, but I remember that he offered me no handout at all, but unloaded his encomiums of him (or her) *viva voce*, and left me to write my own advance notice. In it I limited the star to a few lines, and devoted the rest of my space to Marcus himself. The local theatre manager protested against this, but Marcus was rather pleased, and sent me a signed photograph of himself in token of the fact.

Of a different type was Punch Wheeler, who had come into the theatre from the circus, and affected the make-up of a Mississippi river gambler of 1875 or thereabout — a loud checked suit, a yellow waistcoat embroidered with roses, and a red satin cravat run through a diamond ring. A little while before this time Punch had been a manager on his own account, operating a fly-by-night opera company in what is now called the Drought Bowl. The star thereof was a Baltimorean named Jerome Sykes, who was later to become a favorite on Broadway. (His best rôle there was that of Foxy Quiller in the musical comedy of the same name: I can still hear his sonorous reading of its tag-line: " ' Aha,' said Foxy Quiller, with a crafty leer! ") When the company started out from New York for the Western steppes there was not enough money in the till to hire a chorus, so Punch had a dozen sightly kickers painted on the back-drop. Anon and anon he would duck ahead of the troupe to arrange its bookings, and in every town he would let the local Frohman name the opera to be played. If the Frohman said " Carmen " or " Il Trovatore " or " The Chimes of Normandy " he would bill the town accordingly, for he had picked up a stock of miscellaneous lithographs in Cincinnati, and was his own billsticker as well as his own advance agent. But no matter what opera was billed, Jerome and his four or five associates, when they got to the town, would sing " The Mascot," for that was the only opera all of them knew.

The audiences out in the sticks seldom protested, for most of them were hearing their first opera, and the brisk, voluptuous tunes of " The Mascot " were very ingratiating. Nor did they object to the fact that the chorus was painted on the scenery, for they assumed that such was the custom in opera. Jerome had a loud voice, and made enough noise to give solid support to the female singers, who shrieked their damndest. The company thus did very well in the cow country, and Punch accumulated so much money that on one or two occasions he actually paid salaries. But when, having got to El Paso, he decided to dip over the Rio Grande into Mexico, he and his poor troupers came suddenly and dramatically to grief, for there was a law in Mexico in those days, passed to fetch phony one-ring circuses, making it a criminal offense to advertise an attraction and then not give it. Punch found out about it when Jerome and the company began to warble "The Mascot," for the Frohman at Juarez had asked for "Carmen," and that is what Punch had billed. In the middle of the first act the Mexican cops closed in, the audience (which knew every note of "Carmen") demanded its money back, and Punch, Jerome and the others were locked up in an adobe jug full of scorpions. Jerome, who knew "Carmen," got out the next day by singing the whole score, including the overture, the choruses, and even the soprano and contralto solos, to the chief of police, and a little while later the chief also turned loose the other singers, as innocent victims of the wicked Punch, but it took Punch himself a week or more to beat the rap, and cost him not only all his cash in hand, but also the costumes and scenery of the company, including the back-drop with the chorus painted on it.

I enjoyed his visit to Baltimore immensely, and gave him a good deal more space than his attraction — an "Uncle Tom" company working its way back to New York from the Deep South — was worth. There was nothing intellectual about him, but he was a very amusing fellow, with an endless saga of adventures in the cause of art. When I asked him, on getting acquainted with him, why he continued to wear his fire-alarm make-up, he said that he had got so used to it that he felt almost naked in ordinary clothes. Sometimes, when he hit a town where he wasn't known, the cops would take him for a three-card monte operator, and set a watch on him. Whenever he noticed a couple of dicks trailing him, he would lead them to the main street of the town, pull out a Bible, and begin preaching salvation to the passersby. He was not, of course, in earnest, but he told me that this satirical whooping of the gospel often made converts, and that he figured he had saved at least two hundred head of rubes from Hell. Once he actually converted one of the dicks tailing him. Another time, somewhere in Tennessee, a committee waited on him to offer him the pastorate of a new Baptist church. He got out of it by saying that he was under a vow to wear his checked coat and embroidered vest all the rest of his life, which wouldn't do, of course, for an ecclesiastic, even in Tennessee.

The undisputed king of theatrical press-agents, in my time, was A. Toxen Worm, a Dane of circular cross-section, immense appetite, and low humor. He usually dined alone, mainly because it was impossible to find anyone who could keep up with his eating, or even watch it without swooning. One Sunday evening, happening to be in Philadelphia, I encountered him in the main dining-room of the Bellevue-Stratford just as he was finishing dinner. In those days a dinner-check running beyond $2 was almost unheard of in America, but I noticed that Toxen's was for $6.70. Moreover, it included no charges for drinks, for, as he told me, his kidneys were acting badly, and he was transiently on the wagon. His last course, as I could see by the debris, was a gigantic ice-cream sculpture covered with spun sugar, of the kind served at wedding breakfasts. Three waiters hung about him, panting. It was one of his quiet Sunday evenings.

But if eating was his principal business in life, practical joking was his recreation, and in his time he pulled off some masterpieces. In his own view, so he once told me, he reached his all-time high in a joke at the expense of an English theatrical manager named Hubert Something-or-other. Hubert was a pleasant fellow, but not too bright: in appearance and manner he came close to realizing what was then the average American's notion of a London clubman. He wore cutaway coats, high Piccadilly collars and pants with bold stripes, and from his neck hung a monocle on a wide black ribbon. His mind leaned toward the literal side, and its operations tended to be deliberate. He was married for a time to a well-known American actress, and accompanied her on the road as her company manager. One night, while she was playing at the Academy of Music in Baltimore, I met him in the lobby, and he began telling me an interminable anecdote about some friend of his — a man he described as one of nature's noblemen. But despite his admiration for the fellow, and their intimacy, he could not recall his name. Finally, he appealed to me for help. "You *must* have met him," he said. "Everybody knows him. He was Miss ——'s second husband, the one just before me."

One day Toxen met him in St. Louis, and found him in a low state of mind. He was homesick, it appeared, for London, and especially for its tranquil society. He tired of the wild boozing of America, and longed for the quiet stimulation of afternoon tea. " Don't worry any more," said Toxen. " I can fix it. How would you like to have tea tomorrow afternoon with a lovely lady and her five beautiful daughters — just the two of us — no mob? " Hubert thought it would be perfect, and the next day he arrayed himself in his best cutaway, bought a gardenia for his buttonhole, and, with Toxen steering, took a hack for the house. It turned out to be a fine old mansion in a quiet side street — somewhat decayed outwardly, to be sure, but very ornate inside. The parlor furniture was massive gilt, and there was a thick red carpet on the floor. Hubert liked his hostess instantly, and was delighted by her five daughters, all of whom seemed, rather curiously, to be of an age. Soon tea was served, and Hubert stood up to drink it, his cup and saucer in hand. The prettiest of the five daughters was in front of him, and he turned upon her his best tea-party chit-chat. She professed to be charmed, and moved closer and closer to him. Finally, she was so close that he took an involuntary step backward — and collided with the stern of her Mamma. " See here, you goddam son-of-a-bitch," roared Mamma, "what in hell do you think this is — a whore house?"

In telling the story, Toxen used to say that Hubert dropped cup and saucer, leaped into the hall, grabbed his hat and stick, and ran all the way back to the hotel. Toxen said that he had had to give the madame and the girls $20 for their entertainment, but declared that it would have been cheap at twice the price. Hubert, of course, said nothing, and after a while skeptics began to allege that Toxen had invented the whole story — that nothing of the sort had ever happened. In order to lay this doubt he re-enacted the show in Philadelphia, with a couple of witnesses invited. The witnesses swore that Hubert actually fell for it all over, and in a large way. This time the madame not only bawled him out, but also cracked a saucer over his head, and the girls ganged on him with loud screams, and gave him the bum's rush.

Toxen indulged himself in many other such jocosities as he traveled the country ahead of theatrical troupes, and as time passed, and his technic improved, they tended to become more and more cruel. Once, in Louisville, he tipped the cops that a fellow agent named Charlie Connolly was an absconding bank cashier from Seattle, and Charlie spent a couple of days in a very uncomfortable jail. Another time he hired a loose girl in Buffalo to swear out a warrant against the most respectable agent on the road, alleging seduction under promise of marriage, though everyone knew that the accused was completely innocent. He did a heavy trade in bogus telegrams, most of them of an alarming character. The Frohman brothers, Charles and Daniel, had a brother named Gus who often went on the road for them, and Toxen sent them frequent messages announcing that Gus was locked up for jumping a board bill, or had married a chorus girl, or broken his leg, or committed suicide. His schemes often showed a macabre flavor. He would call up the cops, and tell them that there had been a murder in some theatre, or he would recruit pallbearers for a man who was still alive, or he would spread the story that a fellow agent had been rushed to hospital with smallpox or delirium tremens.

All this went on for years, and there was naturally a considerable accumulation of soreness. In the end the boys combined against Toxen, and resolved to give him a massive dose out of his own bottle. The scene was Denver, and he fell quite easily, for one of his weaknesses was vanity. Thus, when the manager of a local theatre told him in confidence that a rich widow of the town, observing him in the lobby, had got mashed on him he saw nothing impossible in it, and when a note arrived the next day, inviting him to call on her, he not only accepted, but began to throw out hints about a conquest. It was quickly arranged that he should wait upon her at her swell apartment on the top floor of Denver's newest and most elegant apartment-house, and he presented himself at the time fixed wearing his best party clothes, elegantly shaved and perfumed, and carrying a bouquet of orchids. When he rang the bell it was opened by a swarthy maid of gigantic size, and he was invited to enter. The instant he did so one of the boys, previously concealed in the hallway, rushed up and locked the door on him.

Toxen remained in that apartment for three days and three nights. It consisted of one small room, a bath and a kitchenette. The maid was an Indian of a mental age of six or seven years and knew only that she was to keep him from escaping, and dole out to him an occasional ham sandwich. There was no fire-escape, and the telephone wires had been cut. During the long watches of the night Toxen slept on the floor, and the maid snored in the kitchen. By day he spent his time trying to devise some means of escape, but he never managed it, for he was afraid to yell for help and the maid grabbed him and threw him every time he tried to pick the lock of the door. As a practical joke it was almost as successful as his own masterpieces, but as a lesson to him it was a complete failure. Two days after the boys liberated him he was busy once more with his bogus telegrams and his phony tips to the cops.

VII

THE TONE ART

[*1903*]

When it was discovered by the music critic of the *Morning Herald*, a little while after I went to work as a cub reporter, that I could play the piano from the printed music and knew how many sharps were in the key of C major, he began borrowing me from the city editor to cover his third-, fourth- and fifth-string concerts, for he was not only a lazy dog but also had a sensitive ear, and it pained him to have to listen to the false notes so often struck at such affairs. As for me, I did not mind them, for my own playing, like Beethoven's, was pretty inaccurate, and my general taste in music was still somewhat low. I got no extra pay for this service, and indeed no allowance of time: all my regular work had to be done before I could go to a concert, and as a result I often arrived late, and heard only the terminal or Cheyne-Stokes tumults of the performers. But when a Summer opera company was in town, or

Sousa's band, or anything else of that loud and hearty order, I usually managed to get, as the phrase then went, a larger load of it, even at the expense of missing two-thirds of a colored murder, or the whole of a Democratic ward meeting. During my first Summer I thus heard the whole répertoire of bad opera from "Cavalleria Rusticana" to "The Chimes of Normandy," not once but three or four times, and in the intervals of this caterwauling I dropped in now and again on half a dozen Italian bands.

These bands were then at the height of their popularity in the United States, and every trolley park had one. They all put on substantially the same programme every night, beginning with one of the more deafening Rossini overtures and ending invariably with "The Star-Spangled Banner," played a couple of tones above the usual key of B flat to show off the trumpets, for the Spanish-American War was only a few years in the past, and patriotism was still bubbling in the national heart. There were two great set pieces that were never missed: indeed, the audiences of the day would have set down an Italian band leader as a fraud if he failed to play them. One was the sextette from "Lucia di Lammermoor," done with all the trumpets and trombones lined up on the apron of the platform, and the other was the anvil chorus from "Il Trovatore," with a row of real anvils in the same place, and a series of electric wires so arranged that big blue sparks were struck off as the gentlemen of the percussion section clouted the anvils with real hammers. For this last effect, of course, the lights were always turned out. It had been invented years before, so I learned long afterward, by the celebrated Patrick Sarsfield Gilmore, the greatest of all American bandmasters, but by the turn of the century he was dead and forgotten, and the wops who worked his masterpiece all claimed credit for it.

They were, in fact, assiduous copy-cats, and whenever one of them hit on anything really new the rest imitated it at once. As a result it was hard to tell one Italian band from another. They not only played the same programme every night; they also wore the same florid uniforms, and their leaders all exhibited the same frantic gestures and the same barbaric hair-cuts. Any leader who, on coming to the coda of a Rossini overture, with its forty or fifty measures of tonic and dominant chords, did not throw his arms about like a maniac and contrive to make his back hair (it was always long and coal black) flap up and down like a loose hatch in a storm, would have seemed extremely strange. As a matter of record, no such leader was known to musical zoölogists — that is, not until I invented one myself.

This was in 1903 or thereabout, after I had been promoted to the office of dramatic editor. In that rôle, as I have said, I was in charge of all advance notices of musical and theatrical shows, and spent a part of every day receiving press-agents. One day a member of the corps dropped in to introduce, according to the custom then prevailing, a band leader who had just come to town, and the leader informed me, as usual, that he had written a Baltimore *Morning Herald* march and proposed to dedicate it to me as a tribute to my national and even international celebrity as a friend of sound music. This, of course, was an old gag, and it made no impression on me. Every Italian leader had a portfolio of dog's-eared marches that he renamed after the principal papers of whatever city he happened to be playing in, and dedicated to such members of the staffs thereof as handled advance notices. I was thus not interested, for at least six other *Morning Herald* marches had been dedicated to me during my first few months in office. But there was something unusually attractive about this last imitator of imitators of imitators, and after the formal ritual was over I invited him to sit down, and asked him how the world was using him.

He was very young, and, as I could quickly see, not too sure of himself. He had come to the United States, he said, in the hope of getting a desk as a clarinetist in a first-rate symphony orchestra, but he found that it was the prevailing theory among the Germans who then conducted all American orchestras that the only good clarinetists were either Frenchmen or Belgians, and so he had been refused even an audition. He had thereupon joined an Italian band at $14.50 a week, and after a little while the *padrone* who owned it, and a dozen others exactly like it, had offered him the baton of one of them, at an advance, I gathered, to not more than $25. It was with this outfit that he had come to Baltimore, and as we got on easy terms he confessed to me that he greatly feared the competition of the six or eight other bands then playing in town, for his own was made up mainly of riffraff.

One of his tuba players, he said, could play only by ear, and was in fact not a musician at all but a barber, and that very morning at rehearsal it had been necessary to fire the second snare-drummer, a Black Hander from Palermo, for trying to disembowel a piccolo player with one of his drum-sticks. This snare-drummer was now threatening to throw a bomb at the opening concert. The only oboist in the band, who had to double in the English horn, was naturally insane, for mental aberration is almost normal among oboists, but he was worse than the common run, for his lunacy took the form of trying to blow the oboe and the English horn at once — a preposterous feat, of no practical use or sense. As for the six trumpet players — the very sinew and substance of a brass band —, three were red-ink drunkards, two were grappo addicts, and the sixth had to wear a false moustache to throw off the police, who suspected him of a trunk murder in Akron, O., and wanted to sweat him.

The woes of this earnest young Italian aroused

my sympathy, for I was young myself in those days and had many tribulations of my own. Unhappily, I could think of no way to help him against that crew of scalawags, for my experience of musicians had already gone far enough to convince me that there was no cure for their eccentricities. Every band leader in America had the same troubles, and also every orchestra conductor, even the most eminent. There was boozing in the Boston Symphony, and gang-wars were not unheard of at the rehearsals of the New York Philharmonic. He would have to take his band as he found it, and content himself with doing his level damndest: the Good Book itself said that angels could do no more. But there was still some chance of giving him help in the field of public relations, and I let my mind play upon the subject while he talked. Eventually I fished up an idea.

Why, I asked him, go on leading an *Italian* band? There were hundreds, and maybe even thousands of them, in the country, and they were all precisely alike, at least in the eyes of their public. Why not start out from the reasonable assumption that that public was more or less fed up with them, and proceed to give it something different? The professor pricked up his ears, and so did the press-agent, and my fancy began to flow freely. Why not have at the fortissimo fans with a *Spanish* band? Why not, indeed? The Spaniards, who had been fiends in human form only a few years ago, were now fast gathering popularity in the United States — a phenomenon that follows all American wars. Nothing had been too evil to say of them while they were butchering Cubans and Filipinos, but the moment Uncle Sam had to take over the job himself they began, in retrospect, to seem innocent and even humane. Spanish singers were returning to the Metropolitan Opera House, and American women were again wearing red and yellow, the Spanish colors.

The leader and his press-agent concurred after only brief hesitation, and soon we were engaged in preparing an announcement. The name of the band, it appeared, was to be the Royal Palace Band and Drum Corps of Madrid. Its leader was Lieut. José de la Vega of the Spanish Army, a son to the commander of the battleship *Vizcaya*, sunk by Schley at Santiago. The lieutenant himself had been present at that engagement as chief bugler of the battleship *Infanta Maria Teresa*, and had been blown overboard by one of Schley's shells, and then rescued by Schley's gallant jackies, and brought to Tampa and nursed back to normalcy by a beautiful American nurse named Miss Mary Smith, and had fallen in love with her and was about to marry her. The press-agent, a competent craftsman, thought of many interesting details, and even the leader, as he heated up, made some useful contributions. When the question of language was adverted to he relieved the press-agent and me by saying that he knew a few words of Spanish — *Cuanto? De quien es esta sombrero? Siento! La cerveza no es buena,* and so on — enough to fool Americans. So far as I was aware, there was only one actual Spaniard in Baltimore, and he was a man of eighty, floored by rheumatism. There were, of course, plenty of Cubans and Porto Ricans, but none of them would speak to a Spanish officer.

The scheme was launched the next week, and to the tune of considerable friendly réclame in the local press. No one, to my knowledge, detected the imposture, not even the critic of the Baltimore *Sunpapers,* who was not let in on the secret. The leader and his men wore the same uniforms that they had been wearing all the while, and played the orthodox programme, with the addition of the *habanera* from " Carmen " and " La Paloma." The only real concession to verisimilitude was offered by the press-agent, who had a large Spanish flag made and hung it behind the band. At the end of the first half of the first concert the large audience leaped to its feet and cheered, and when the last note of the evening was played there was so vociferous a demand for encores that Lieut. de la Vega did " La Paloma " twice more, the second time *pianissimo* with the lights dimmed. During the intermission I encountered one of the professors at the Peabody Conservatory of Music, and he told me that he was greatly enjoying the evening. Italian bands, he said, drove him wild, but the Spaniards at least knew how to get decent sounds out of the woodwind. "If this fellow," he said, "would sneak in four or five Italian trumpet players he would have a really good band."

Unhappily, the innovation, though an artistic success, was killed in its infancy by the Italian *padrone* who owned the band. When he heard that it had gone Spanish he raised a considerable pother, mainly on prudential grounds. If the news ever got to Italy, he said, he would be disgraced forever, and the Black Hand would probably murder his old mother. Moreover, he was presently reinforced by the members of the band, and especially by the gorilla moiety thereof. They demanded an immediate raise of $2 a week as compensation for the infamy of being turned into Spaniards, and when it was refused they took to sabotage. On the opening night of the second week, when the time came to launch the first dose of "La Paloma," the whole band began to play "Funiculi-Funicula" instead, greatly to Lieut. de la Vega's astonishment and chagrin. There was, of course, nothing for him to do save go along, but during the intermission he gave the performers a piece of his mind, and they responded by threatening to plant a bomb under his podium. Before the end of that second week the band was demanding a raise of $4, and the *padrone* came to Baltimore to make peace. The upshot was that in return for a solemn promise to let his old mother in Naples live he burned the Spanish flag, fired the press-agent, and ordered Lieut. de la Vega to resume the style and appelation of Antonio Bracciolini, which he had been before. A little while later the band gave place to another from the same stable, and in the course of time, I suppose, it succumbed to the holocaust which engulfed all the Italian bands in America. I never heard from Lieut. de la Vega-Bracciolini again. But now and then I got news of the press-agent. He was going about the country telling newspaper colleagues that I was a smartie who deserved a kick in the pants.

I got to know a good many other musicians in those days, and found many of them pleasant fellows, though their ways of life were strange. I well recall a talented lady pianist who came to Baltimore for six seasons running, and each time brought a new husband, always of a new nationality. The last that I saw was a Turk, and afterward, so I have heard, she proceeded to a Venezuelan, a South African Dutchman and a native of Monte Carlo, but on that point I can't speak from personal knowledge. I also remember a French tenor who traveled with no less than three wives, but that was before the passage of the Mann Act. Two of them sang in the chorus of his company, and while they were on the stage the third took care of their and her own infants in the baggage-room. This company had come up from South America, and carried on its affairs according to provincial Italian principles. Everything was sung in the fashion of the sextette in "Lucia" — that is, with the singers in a long row at the footlights. This was done even in the final agonies of "Traviata," with *Violette* dying of tuberculosis. As the curtain fell the lady playing the rôle — she weighed at least 200 pounds — was lined up with *Alfred, Annina, Germont* and *Dr. Grenvil,* howling *Gran Dio! morir si giovane!* (Great God! to die so young!) in a voice of brass. One warm evening, approaching the opera-house somewhat late, I could hear the screams of the polygamous tenor two blocks away. He was throwing a lot of violent and supernumerary high C's, many of them *sforzando,* into *Deserto sulla terra.*

I soon found that, among the instrumental players, the register of the instrument apparently had some effect upon the temperament of the artist. The bull-fiddle players were solid men who played the notes set before them, however difficult, in a dogged and uncomplaining manner, and seldom gave a conductor any trouble, whether by alcoholism or Bolshevism. The cellists were also pretty reliable fellows, but in the viola section one began to encounter boozers, communists and even spiritualists, and when one came to the fiddlers it was reasonable to expect anything, including even a lust to maim and kill. So, also, in the brass and woodwind. No one ever heard of a bassoon or tuba player saying or doing anything subversive, but the trumpeters were vain and quarrelsome, the flautists and clarinetists were often heavy drinkers, and the oboists, as I have noted, were predominantly *meshug-*

gah. Learning these instructive facts, I began to have some sympathy with orchestra conductors, a class of men I had hitherto dismissed as mere athletes, comparable to high-jumpers, circus acrobats and belly-dancers. I now realized that their lives were full of misery, and when, a few years later, I became well acquainted with a number of them, it seemed only natural to learn that they were steady readers of Schopenhauer and Nietzsche and heavy consumers of aspirin, mineral oil and bicarbonate of soda.

Indeed, my gradually growing familiarity with musicians taught me many interesting things about them, and also helped my comprehension of the general mystery of man. It did not surprise me to discover that a great many of them, in their professional capacity, hated music, for I was already aware that most bartenders of any sense were teetotalers and that some of the most eminent medical men at the Johns Hopkins Hospital took patent medicines when they were ill, but it *did* surprise me to find that this animosity to the tone art as a trade was often accompanied by a deep love of it as a recreation. I well recall my delight when I was invited by a Baltimore brewer to a party at his brewery in honor of a dozen members of the Boston Symphony Orchestra, and saw them strip off their coats and fall upon a stack of chamber music that kept them going until 4 a.m. These men, all of whom were first-rate performers, had put in the early part of the evening playing a heavy concert, with a new tone-poem by Richard Strauss, bristling with technical snares, as its principal ingredient. They agreed unanimously that Strauss was a scoundrel, that his music was an outrage upon humanity, and that anyone who paid good money to hear it was insane. Yet these same men, after nearly two hours of professional suffering, now spent four more hours playing for the pleasure of it, and one of the things they played with the greatest gusto was Strauss's serenade in E flat for wind instruments, opus 7. All they got for their labor, save for a keg of beer to each man and the applause of the brewer and of the customers he had invited to meet them, was a hot inner glow, obviously extremely grateful. As I sat listening to them I could not help pondering upon the occult satisfaction that arises from the free and perfect performance of a function, as when a cow gives milk or a dog chases a cat. If the stars were sentient they would no doubt get the same kick out of their enormous revolutions, otherwise so pointless. These reflections, in some way or other, induced me to resume music myself, abandoned since my boyhood, and I was presently playing trios and quartettes with an outfit that devoted four hours of every week to the job — that is, two hours to actual playing and the other two to the twin and inseparable art of beer-drinking.

The members of this little club were all very

much better performers than I was, and it puzzled me at the start to find them so tolerant of my inferiority. I discovered the secret when, after a little while, they took in a recruit even worse, for I was a good deal less pained by the dreadful sounds he made than cheered by his pious enthusiasm. In brief, he really loved music, and that was enough to excuse a great many false entrances and sour notes. I could stand him, at least up to a point, just as the rest could stand me, again up to a point. That club goes on to the present day, though I am the only survivor of the era of my own admission. It has included through the years some first-rate professionals and it has also included some amateurs hardly worth shooting, but they have got on together very amicably, and though they are now mainly elderly men, with kidneys like sieves, they still meet once a week, Winter or Summer, in war-time or peace-time, rain or shine. From end to end of World War I an Englishman sat between two Germans at every meeting, and in World War II a Czech has his place, and two Jews flank the Germans. What this signifies I refrain, on the advice of counsel, from venturing to suggest: in all probability it is downright unlawful. But there it is.

The club, in its day, has had some men of more or less note among its members, and there were times during its earlier stages when the question of honorifics presented a certain difficulty. Should a distinguished university, governmental or ecclesiastical dignitary be addressed by his simple surname or given his title? In the case of those who sat regularly the problem was soon solved in the Rotarian fashion by calling him Julius or Charlie, but when he came only occasionally it was got round by giving him a satirical lift. Thus a plain Mister became Doctor, a Doctor became Professor, and a Professor became *Geheimrat*. If there had ever been a colonel in the club we'd have made him a general, and if there had ever been an archbishop we'd have addressed him as Your Eminence or perhaps even Your Holiness. Once, when a baron sat in for a few sessions, we called him Count, and another time we promoted a judge to Mr. Chief Justice. The club has always had a few non-performing members, but they have been suffered only on condition that they never make any suggestions about programmes or offer any criticism of performances. The same rule has applied to occasional guests: they are welcome if they keep their mouths shut and do not sweat visibly when the flute is half a tone higher than the first violin, but not otherwise. The club has never gone on the air or had its disturbances recorded on wax, but nevertheless it has done more than one humble service to the tone art, and in the dark forward and abysm of the future those services may be acknowledged and even rewarded. For one thing, it has produced, from its composers' section, at least one peerless patriotic hymn, to wit, "I Am a 100% American," by William W. Woollcott. This magnificent composition has everything. It is both chaste and voluptuous. It radiates woof and it reeks with brrrrrrrr. I am frankly tender toward it, for when the inspiration for it seized the composer I had the honor of taking it down at the piano: he was, at the moment, suffering from a sprained arm, and moreover, he plays no instrument save the triangle, and that only in a dilettante fashion. A print of it exists and may be found in libraries, but so far it has not got its deserts from the public. Perhaps it will take a third World War or even a fourth to bring it out. National hymns, as everyone knows, sometimes linger a long while in the dog-house before they win universal acceptance and acclaim. Even "The Star-Spangled Banner" was formally adopted by Congress only a few years ago; indeed, it outran "God Bless America" by hardly more than a neck.

But the greatest of all of Willie Woollcott's inspirations was his plan to play the first eight Beethoven symphonies seriatim, with only brief halts for refreshments between them. He omitted the Ninth only because the club's singing section, at that time, lacked castrati, and in fact consisted of but two men, both of them low, growling basses. We had excellent arrangements of the first eight symphonies, and after debating the project for two or three years resolved at last to give Willie's bold project a whirl. This must have been in 1922 or thereabout, when the club had the largest membership in its history, including a great many bold and reckless men, some of them aviators or ex-marines. Willie not only supplied the idea; he also proposed to supply the scene — his house in a dense woods near Baltimore, with no neighbors within earshot — and the refreshments. It seemed a reasonable arrangement, and so we fell to — at 4 o'clock of a Summer afternoon.

The First Symphony was child's play to us, and we turned it off in record time, with a pause of only ten minutes afterward. By six o'clock we had also finished the Second, and then we stopped for cocktails and dinner. After dinner there was some relaxation, and we dallied a bit with some excellent malt liquor, so that it was eight o'clock before we tackled the Eroica. It began so badly that we played the first movement twice, but after that it picked up momentum, and by 9.30 we had finished it. Then we paused again, this time for sandwiches, a walk in the woods — it was a lovely moonlit night — and another resort to the malt, but at 11.30 or maybe a little later we were back in the trenches, and the Fourth was begun. For some reason or other it went even worse than the Eroica, though it actually makes much less demand on technic, and the clock must have been near to 1 a.m. when we decided finally that it had been done well enough. Our struggles with it had naturally tired us, so we decided to knock off for an hour and find out what the malt had to offer in the way of encouragement.

This hiatus, unhappily, was a fatal one, for when the time came to resume the hullabaloo it was discovered that two of the members had sneaked off for home, and that two more were so sound asleep that we could not arouse them without risk of hurting them. Thus the C minor was begun under unfavorable circumstances, and by the time it was over the band was reduced to what amounted to a mere fragment, and the four-hand piano was making so much noise that the other surviving instruments were barely audible. The Pastoral followed at once, but how it was done I can't say, for I fell asleep myself somewhere in the *scherzo*, and by the time Willie got me back on the piano bench the end had been reached and there was a debate going on about No. 7. It was now nearly 5 a.m., and the east was rosy with the dawn. One faction, it appeared, was in favor of giving up and going home; another insisted that a round of ham and eggs and a few beers would revive us enough to take us to the end. As to what actually happened there are two legends. The official story, inscribed by Willie upon the scrolls of the club, is that we tackled the Seventh, banged through it in circus time, and then dispatched the Eighth. A rump account says that we blew up in the middle of the Seventh, leaped to the Eighth, blew up again, and were chased out by our host, assisted by his hunting dogs. According to this rump account, but three performers were left at the end — the *primo* pianist, one fiddler and a man trying to play a basset-horn.

My own feeling is that in such bizarre matters precise facts are only intrusions. If we actually played the eight symphonies, then no other group of *Tonkünstler* has ever done it, on this or any other earth. And if we only tried, then no one else has ever tried.

VIII

A MASTER OF

GLADIATORS

[*1907*]

It always amazes me how easily men of the highest talents and eminence can be forgotten in this careless world — for example, the late Abraham Lincoln Herford, manager of the incomparable Joe Gans, lightweight champion of the world. Even Joe himself, though he was probably the greatest boxer who ever lived and unquestionably one of the gamest, is mentioned only rarely by the sporting writers, and in his native Baltimore there is no memorial to him save a modest stone in an Aframerican graveyard, far off the usual lines of tourist travel. It may be that pilgrims occasionally visit it, but if so they have to use large-scale maps, showing every culvert and hot-dog stand. Joe's funeral was a stupendous event, with services running seriatim in three different churches, ten or twelve choirs moaning sad music, and no colored Baltimorean absent who could get the afternoon off and squeeze in, but since then the dead gladiator's fellow blackamoors have let his memory fade, and gone flocking after newer and lesser heroes. There is no Gans boulevard, avenue, street or even alley in the Harlem of Baltimore, and no Gans park. Some years ago I heard talk of raising a monument to Joe in Perkins Square, hard by his humble birthplace, with a marble effigy of him in ring costume on top of it, but the scheme faded out as all plans and projects among the colored people have a way of doing. If it is ever revived I hope to be invited to participate, for my admiration for Joe was high while he lived and has not abated since his decease. Specifically, I offer herewith to contribute $100 in cash money whenever a sufficiently reliable committee opens subscription books. By reliable, of course, I do not mean one certified by the S.E.C. or by a gang of colored pastors or gamblers, but one certified by the Baltimore cops.

But if Joe was great, then Al Herford must have been great also, for he grasped Joe's genius when it was still occult to other men, and nursed it to flower with both skill and tenderness. Of Al's origins I know nothing, for I did not become acquainted with him until he was already well up in the world, and president *and* treasurer of the Eureka Athletic and Social Club. Under the laws prevailing in Maryland in those days, it was forbidden to give boxing exhibitions for hire, but any group of fans was free to form a club to stage them in private, and that is what the Eureka brethren did, with Al acting as their agent and adviser. Their meetings were held every Friday evening at the old Germania Maennerchor hall in Lombard street, and ran about three hours, with a fifteen-round bout at the end, usually between heavyweights. According to the by-laws of the club each member paid his weekly dues as he came in, and the rate for those who wanted seats near the ring was considerably higher than for those who were content to sit in the gallery. Al always opened the proceedings by reading the minutes of the last meeting. They described briefly the bouts that had entertained the members, and then went on to a technical commentary upon them, frequently of great acuteness. If there had been any distinguished new members present, say a party of Congressmen from Washington, Al recited their names, and bade them welcome to the club. At the end of the minutes he called for motions from the floor, and some member always moved that the club make up a purse and buy the president *and* treasurer a diamond ring or stick-pin. Al handed over the gavel, at this point, to Ernie Gephart, who was secretary and time-keeper of the club, but after the motion had been put and carried (as it was invariably, and unanimously) he returned long enough to announce that subscriptions might be paid to the doorkeeper on the way out.

Al never bored the members with financial statements, though he always stressed the *and* in " president *and* treasurer," for the by-laws made them virtually supererogatory. According to Article II all the money collected in dues went into a pot in the custody of the president *and* treasurer, and out of it he paid all the necessary expenses of the meetings — for example, for hall rent, announcements in the newspapers, stationery and postage, the fees of the sporty young doctor who served as the club's surgeon, and the honoraria of the pugs invited to exhibit their art. If anything was left over, which was usually the case, it was given to the president *and* treasurer, as a small return for his services. This simple system worked beautifully, and had the approval of the Baltimore cops. They came to the meetings in large numbers, and were so well appreciated by the other members that the doorkeeper, by a tacit but general understanding, always forgot to collect their dues. Sometimes, when a couple of extra-fat captains were present at the ringside, Al would have a little fun with them by announcing that they would go on for six rounds at the next meeting. He also had a line of spoofing for visitors from Washington, and did not hesitate to refer to the most puissant Senators, and even judges, by their Christian names. The other members were delighted to belong to a club which included so many illustrious men. More than once I have sat at the ringside with a Senator or Governor to either side of me, and two or three stars of the Federal judiciary just behind.

Al was not only president *and* treasurer of the club, but also its announcer, and his introductions always showed an exuberant fancy. When two colored flyweights were brought on for a preliminary he presented them as Young Terry McGovern of San Francisco and Young Joe Gans of Australia. Nearly everyone knew, of course, that they were actually water-boys from the Pimlico racetrack, but the members liked Al's style, and always professed to believe him. His humor was protean, and never flagged. When two boys sailed into each other with unusual vehemence and the members began to howl, he would signal Ernie Gephart to let the rounds run on, and whenever, on the contrary, a bout was tame, he would cut them short. Once I saw a set-to between two ferocious colored youths, Young Corbett, of Yarmouth, England, and the Zulu Whirlwind, of Cape Town, South Africa, in which the average length of the five rounds, by actual timing, was twelve and a half minutes, and another time I saw Ernie put through a flabby six-round bout in ten minutes flat, with the pauses for wind, massage and hemostasis included.

Al was very inventive, and many of his innovations stuck. He was, I believe, the first announcer in Europe or America to call the penultimate bout of an evening the semi-windup. I recall that some of the more literate members of the Eureka Club snickered at the neologism, and that I was brought up by it myself. But in a little while it had swept the boxing world, and it is now used without any thought of vulgarity by such purists as John F. Kieran and Grantland Rice. Al, a little later, began to call the second from the last bout the semi-semi-windup, and the third from the last the semi-semi-semi-windup, but these innovations never took, and he proceeded no further. He did not invent the battle-royal, but I believe it is only just to say that he greatly developed it. One of his contributions was the scheme of dividing the four boys into three very small ones and one very tall one: this favored a brisk entertainment, for the dwarfs always ganged on the giant and knocked him out, usually by blows behind the ear. Another of Al's improvements was the device of dressing the colored boys who fought in battles-royal, not in ordinary trunks, but in the billowy white drawers that women then wore. The blacker the boy, the more striking the effect. In all such massacres, of course, the scheme of holding back time on a good round was carried out. So long as the members kept on guffawing and hollering Al let the boys clout away.

Al, in his private life, was a very generous fellow, but in his character of president *and* treasurer of the club he kept a sharp eye on its funds. The standard fee for preliminary boys of no experience was $4, win or lose, but he seldom paid it without a struggle, which meant that he seldom paid it at all. Once, after a long evening marked by extraordinary carnage, I sat with him in his bureau under the stage while the boys came in to collect their money. I recall a pair of young featherweights who could barely stand up — Young Jeffries, of Honolulu, and Young Fitzsimmons, of Yale University. Both of Jeffries' eyes were blacked, his nose was only a squash, and he claimed that he had broken all five fingers of his right hand. The Yale boy had been used even worse, and when I entered the bureau the club surgeon was giving him a ticket to the free surgical clinic at the University of Maryland Hospital. They had fought six really terrific rounds, and the club referee, Jim O'Hara, had let them go on after the fourth only because he could not make out which was getting the worse beating. But Al conceived it to be his duty as treasurer of the club to challenge them, and challenge them he did. " What! " he roared. " Have you bastards the nerve to come down here and talk of money after doing a *brother* act? Do you think this place is a dancing-school? Back to the Y.M.C.A., and fight with feather-pillows! I could sue you in the courts. I could sick the cops on you. Never let me see you again. Here [to Jeffries] is two dollars, and here [to Fitzsimmons de Yale] is a dollar and a half. Now scram before I get mad and kick you to hell out of here."

On this occasion, unhappily, Al went a shade too far, for the next day he was waited on by Lawyer Melville W. Fuller Fineblatt, secretary of the Central Police Court Bar Association, and forced to disgorge. Lawyer Fineblatt not only collected the balance of the four dollars that was due to each boy under the rules, but also three dollars a head for medical expenses, and a fee of twenty dollars for himself. The alternative to coughing up, he said firmly, would be a prosecution for violating the laws against giving public boxing exhibitions, allowing smoking in a theatre, maintaining a nuisance, embezzling trust funds, and contributing to the delinquency of minors. Al entered a long and indignant account of the episode in the minutes, and read it at the next meeting of the club, but when he came to the statement that the boys had put on a fake some of the members began to laugh, and he pursued the matter no further. But he continued to labor it *in petto,* and nine or ten years later, after public boxing exhibitions had become lawful in Maryland and the Eureka Athletic and Social Club had withered away, he was still talking darkly of having Lawyer Fineblatt disbarred.

How much he made out of Joe Gans, first and last, I can't tell you, for he kept his books in his hat, but I knew the man, and am morally certain that he never collared more than fifty percent, or maybe sixty percent, of Joe's earnings. If this seems a large cut, then don't forget that many of the other pug managers of the time took seventy percent, and even eighty; indeed, there were some who took all, less enough, of course, to victual their boys, and keep them housed and clothed. Joe's own share was surely considerable, for when he retired from the ring for the first of his fifteen times he had saved enough to open a gaudy night-club in Baltimore — the first black-and-tan resort the town had ever seen. To be sure, it blew up quickly, and Joe died in a low state, financially speaking, but nevertheless the money he lost had passed through his hands.

Al taught him a lot, not only about the business of boxing, but also about the carriage and conduct of a professional man, and Joe became widely known as the most gentlemanly pugilist then on earth. His manners were those of a lieutenant of the guards in old Vienna, and many managers sent their white boys to him to observe and learn. When he was shoveled away at last, Al undertook the tutelage of a colored boxer named Young Peter Jackson, a heavyweight. Peter was an apt pupil, and soon became famous for his elegance. Unhappily, he lacked Joe's natural grace, and was in fact a squat, clumsy fellow with a coal-black hide and a shaven head. Once he made a tour of England under the eye of an English manager named Jolly Jumbo, and the sports were so delighted by his suave ways that, on his return to America, they chipped in money for a farewell present. Jolly

Jumbo was deputed to select it. Forgetting Peter's depilated poll, he chose a set of gold-mounted military brushes.

Another of Al's protégés (in his announcements and harangues to the club he always pronounced the word pro-teege) was a heavyweight who shined for a brief season, but then took to heavy eating and lost his wind, and eventually got so dreadful a beating from Philadelphia Jack O'Brien that he retired from the ring and opened a saloon. I was present at his Waterloo, sitting with my knees touching the ropes, and remember it because of the poor fellow's extraordinary loss of blood, chiefly from his nose. Directly beside me sat Judge John H. Anderson, sporting editor of the *Morning Herald* and the first Harvard Phi Beta Kappa man ever to occupy such a position. The judge, who had got his title, not on the bench but at the race-track, wore a round beard *à la* James A. Garfield, and was extremely dignified and even formal in appearance and manner. I well recall his profane protests when the unhappy heavyweight's gore began to sprinkle his beard. He did not object to the rosin dust that overspread it at every meeting of the club, nor even to an occasional drop of blood, but when great gouts began to hit his foliage he set up a hell of an uproar, and if the heavyweight had not gone to the mat a little while later I have no doubt that he would have forced Al to stop the bout. When the Prohibition infamy hit the country in 1920 the heavyweight converted his saloon into a speakeasy, and was soon raided by Federal agents. The first jury acquitted him, for it was made up largely of members of Al's old club, and so did the second, third, fourth, fifth, sixth, seventh and eighth. But on his ninth appearance the district attorney took precautions, and he was duly found guilty and sentenced to three months in jail. While he was cooped there he was allowed to have his meals sent in from outside, and in a couple of weeks his gluttony had reduced him to such a state that he needed medical advice. He thereupon asked and was given permission to send for one of the visiting physicians of the Johns Hopkins Hospital — a very skillful and high-toned consultant. Simultaneously, he read in the Baltimore *Sunpaper* that his favorite niece, a pretty girl then in the foolish stage of her life, had been nabbed as a witness to a roughhouse in a rowdy suburban night-club. This smudge upon the honor of his house affected him deeply, and when the doctor waited upon him at the jail he was actually in tears. "My God, doctor," he moaned, "just think of it, just think of it! I been so ashamed to look anybody in the eye that for two days I ain't been out of my cell."

IX

A DIP INTO

STATECRAFT

[*1912*]

SOME time ago, in writing a book for the edification of the young, I let fall the remark that, in the now forgotten year of 1912, I was a candidate for the Democratic nomination for Vice-President of the United States. It is almost incredible that an author of my experience should have made such a slip. I must have been very well aware, even in the cachexia of composition, that the only effect of my statement would be to provoke a storm of snorts, and get me classed among the damndest liars on earth. That, indeed, is exactly what happened, and during the month after the book came out (it had a very fair sale) I received 30,000 or 40,000 letters full of hoots and sneers. Nevertheless, my statement was true in the most precise and literal sense, and I hereby reiterate it with my hand upon the Holy Scriptures. I was actually a candidate as I said, but I should add at once, before historians begin to rush up with their proofs, that I did not get the nomination.

Perhaps the best way to tell the story, which is mercifully brief, will be to start out with a cast of characters. Here it is:

The Hon. J. Harry Preston, mayor of Baltimore, and a man of aggressive and relentless bellicosity.

Charles H. Grasty, editor of the Baltimore *Sunpapers*, an enemy to Preston, and a sly and contriving fellow.

H. L. Mencken, a young journalist in the employ of Grasty as columnist and trigger-man.

Scene: Baltimore.

Time: The weeks preceding the Democratic National Convention of 1912.

That was the year when the late Woodrow Wilson was nominated and so began his dizzy rise to immortality. Grasty was for him, but Preston was against him and in favor of Champ Clark of Missouri. This difference was only one of hundreds that lay between them. They quarreled all the time, and over any proposition that could be dissected into alternatives. If Preston, as mayor, proposed to enlarge the town dog-pound, Grasty denounced it in both morning and evening *Sunpapers* as an assault upon the solvency of Baltimore, the comity of nations, and the Ten Commandments, and if Grasty argued in the *Sunpapers* that the town alleys ought to be cleaned oftener Preston went about the ward clubs warning his heelers that the proposal was only the opening wedge for anarchy, atheism and cannibalism. It was impossible to unearth anything against Preston's private character, though every *Sun* reporter, under Grasty's urging, made desperate efforts to do so, for he was a respectable family man, a vestryman in an Episcopal church with a watchful rector, and a lawyer of high standing at the bar. But in his rôle of politician, of course, he was an easier target, and so his doings in the City Hall were gradually assimilated (at least in the *Sunpapers*) to those of Tweed in New York, the *ancien régime* in France, and the carpetbaggers in the South.

Grasty, on his side, was vulnerable in the reverse order. That is to say, he could not be accused of political corruption, for it was notorious that he had no political ambitions, but in his private life there was more encouraging material, for several times, in the past, he had forgotten himself. The dirt thus dredged up was gradually amalgamated into the master charge that he had been run out of Kansas City (where he formerly lived) for a series of adulteries of a grossly levantine and brutal nature. This charge Preston not only labored at great length in his harangues to the ward clubs; he also included it in his commencement addresses to the graduates of the Baltimore high-schools and his speeches of welcome to visiting Elks, Shriners,

Christian Endeavorers and plumbers' supply dealers; moreover, he reduced it to writing, signed his name to it with a bold flourish, and printed it as paid advertising in the *Sunpapers* themselves.

The revenues from this advertising were gratefully received by Grasty, for the *Sunpapers*, in those days, were using up almost as much red ink in the business office as printer's ink in the pressroom. But against that pleasant flow of the wages of sin there had to be set off the loss from the municipal advertising, which Preston, though a Democrat, diverted to a Republican paper. It took him a long while to clear it out of the *Sunpapers*, but clear it out he did at last. Any City Hall functionary who, by force of old habit, sent in an announcement of a tax sale or a notice of an application to open a hat-cleaning parlor was fired forthwith and to the tune of loud screams of indignation. To meet this devastating attack the whole staff of the two *Sunpapers* spent half its time in concocting reprisals. No story against Preston was too incredible to be printed, and no criticism too trivial or irresponsible. If the blackamoors in the death-house at the Baltimore City Jail had signed a round robin accusing him of sending them poison in cornpone or snuff, it would have gone into type at once.

My own share in this campaign of defamation was large and assiduous. In my daily column on the editorial page of the *Evening Sun* I accused Preston of each and every article in my private catalogue of infamies. Once I even alleged that he was a Sunday-school superintendent — and was amazed to discover that it was true. I had nothing against him personally; on the contrary, I was fond of him, thought he was doing well as mayor, and often met him amicably at beer-parties. But in his character of enemy of Grasty, and hence of the *Sunpapers*, I was bound by the journalistic code of the time to deal him a lick whenever I could, and this I did every day. On some days, in fact, my whole column was devoted to reviling him. Why he never hit back by accusing me of adultery, or, at all events, of fornication, I do not know, but no doubt it was because he was too busy amassing and embellishing his case against Grasty.

The plain people of Baltimore naturally took his side against the *Sunpapers*. They are always, in fact, against newspapers, and they are always in favor of what reformers call political corruption. They believe that it keeps money in circulation, and makes for a spacious and stimulating communal life. Thus they cheered Preston every time he appeared in public, and especially did they cheer him every time the *Sunpapers* published fresh allegations that he and his goons, having made off with everything movable in the City Hall, were beginning on the slate roof and the doorknobs. This popularity had a powerful effect on the man himself, for he was not without the vanity that afflicts the rest of us. He began to see himself as a great tribune of the people, ordained by God to rescue them from the entrapments of a dissolute journalism, by libel out of crim. con. More, he began to wonder if the job of mayor of Baltimore was really large enough for his talents. Wasn't there something grander and juicier ahead? Didn't the Bible itself guarantee that a good and faithful servant should have a reward? What if the people of Maryland should decide to draft the man who had saved the people of Baltimore, and make him their Governor and Captain-General? What if the people of the whole United —

But this last wayward thought had to wait until, early in 1912, the Democrats of the nation decided that Baltimore should be their convention city. Preston, as mayor, had a large hand in bringing the party national committee to that decision. He not only made eloquent representations about the traditional delights of the town, especially in the way of eating and drinking; he also agreed to raise a fund of $100,000 to pay the costs of the show, and made a big contribution to it himself, for he was a man of means. During the Spring the wild fancies and surmises that were devouring him began to emerge. One day the Republican paper getting the city advertising suggested that he would make a magnificent candidate for the Vice-Presidency, the next day he received hundreds of spontaneous letters and telephone calls from his jobholders, urging him to accept the plain call of his country, and the third day his campaign was in the open, and throwing out dense clouds of sparks and smoke. It soon appeared that he had an understanding with Champ Clark. Clark had already rounded up a majority of the delegates to the coming convention, but he needed more, for the two-thirds rule still prevailed. Why couldn't the Baltimore gallery, packed and fomented by Preston, panic enough waverers to give Clark the nomination? It seemed an enlightened trade, and it was made. If Preston delivered the goods and Clark became the standard-bearer, Preston would have second place.

It was at this point that Grasty conceived his hellish plot, and the rest of the story is soon told. Under the presidential primary law then on the books in Maryland every candidate for the Presidency who itched for the votes of the state's delegates had to file his name " before the first Monday in May " preceding the convention, and with it deposit $270 in cash money. Under the same law candidates for the Vice-Presidency lay under the same mulct. If no candidate submitted to it, the state convention was free to instruct the delegates to the national convention to vote for anyone it fancied, but if there were two who had paid up it had to make its choice between them, and if there was but one it had to instruct the delegates to vote for him. The agents of Wilson, Clark and all the other contenders for first place on the ticket had entered their appearances and paid their fees, but no candidate for the Vice-Presidency had been heard from. Preston, of course, knew the law, but he was a thrifty fellow and saw no reason why he should waste $270, for he figured with perfect plausibility that he would be the only aspirant for second place before the state convention.

Grasty's sinister mind grasped this point a day or two before I was sailing for Europe on a holiday. Summoned to his office, I sat enchanted while he unfolded his plan. It was to wait until the very last minute for filing names of Vice-Presidential candidates, and then rush an agent to Annapolis, properly equipped with $270 in cash, to file *mine.* "Go back to your office," he instructed me, "and write a letter of acceptance. Say in it that you are sacrificing yourself to save the country from the menace of Preston. Lay it on with a shovel, and take all the space you want. To be sure, you'll be in the middle of the Atlantic when the time comes, but I'll send you a wireless, so you'll know what to say when the New York *Herald* reporter meets you at Cherbourg. The joke will wreck Preston, and the shock may even kill him. If he actually shoots himself I'll tone down your statement a bit, but write it as if he were still alive and howling. Imagine the scene when the state convention is forced to instruct the delegates to the national convention to vote for you! Here is the law: read it and laugh. It is really too rich, especially this point: the delegates to the national convention will have to vote for you *as a unit* until 'in their conscientious judgment' you are out of the running. That may not come until days and even weeks after the convention starts. All the Wilson men will throw you votes to annoy Clark. Now get busy with your letter of acceptance before I laugh myself to death."

On the fatal evening I was aboard ship in lat. 50 N, long. 15 W, gulping down beer with my traveling companion, A. H. McDannald, another *Sunpaper* man, and keeping a sharp lookout for a page-boy with a radio envelope. McDannald was in on the plot, and helped me to itch and pant. We got through beer after beer — one, two, three, six, ten, *n*. We wolfed plate after plate of sandwiches. We returned to beer. We ordered more sandwiches. The hours moved on leaden feet; the minutes seemed to be gummy and half dead. Finally, we were the only passengers left in the smokeroom, and the bartender and waiters began to shuffle about pointedly and to douse the lights. Just as darkness closed in on us the page-boy came at last. He had two messages for McDannald and three for me. Both of McDannald's read "Sorry to have missed you; bon voyage," and so did two of mine. The third read: "Everything is off. Say nothing to anyone."

It was not until I got home, four weeks later, that I found out what had happened. Grasty, it appeared, had been so taken by the ingenuity and villainy of his scheme that when he went to the Maryland Club the next afternoon for his daily ration of Manhattan cocktails he couldn't resist revealing it — in strict confidence, of course — to one of the bibuli there assembled. I should say that the bibulus was normally a very reliable man, and carried in his breast a great many anecdotes of Grasty that Preston would have given gold and frankincense to hear, but this time he was so overcome by the gorgeousness of the secret that he took a drop too much, and so blabbed. This blabbing was done in the sanctity of the club, but Preston had his spies even there. Thus, when Grasty's agent appeared at the office of the Secretary of State at Annapolis, at the very last minute for filing names, with $270 in greenbacks held tightly in his fist, it was only to find that Preston's agent had got there two minutes before him, and was engaged with snickers and grimaces in counting out the same sum.

I thereby missed my purple moment, and maybe even immortality. Now that the facts are before a candid world, let the publicists of the *Nation*, the *New Masses* and the *New Republic* speculate upon the probable effects upon history — nay, upon the very security and salvation of humanity — if Grasty's scheme had worked. I offer them the job without prejudice, for no matter how powerfully their minds play upon it their verdict will be only moot. It was not until years later that I discovered that the Constitution of the United States, Article II, Section 1, provides that no person shall be eligible for the Presidency, and *pari passu* for the Vice-Presidency, "who shall not have attained to the age of thirty-five years." On that July day of 1912 when the Hon. Thomas R. Marshall of Indiana got my job I was precisely thirty-one years, ten months and twenty-three days old — and the Constitution was still in force.

X

COURT OF HONOR

[*1913*]

ONE of the oldest of legal wheezes is to the effect that no man should sit as judge in his own case. You will find it in the "Sententiae" of Publilius Syrus, written in the First Century B.C., and it must have been ancient when Publilius lifted it — as he lifted everything else — from some forgotten Greek. In all the years since his time no one, so far as I can discover, has ever ventured to dispute it. It is one of the few propositions that Leftists and Rightists agree on, and even judges on the bench — or, at all events, those among them who give their dismal trade any thought at all — speak well of it. But is it really true? Sometimes I find myself in doubt, just as I sometimes find myself in doubt that two and two are four, or that Jonah actually swallowed the whale. Especially do these wayward misgivings beset me when my memory plays with a case of extra-legal adultery that I became privy to in New York City in the year 1912. In that case one and the same man was not only both judge and complainant, but also prosecuting attorney, yet the verdict that he handed down was fair, equitable and just, and the sentence that he pronounced was notably humane.

Needless to say, he was not a common or dirt judge, deteriorated and debauched by years of listening to lying witnesses and nefarious lawyers. He was not even, in fact, a man of any learning in the law: he was simply a theatrical manager, and even more ignorant than most of them are. He kept an office in the heart of the theatrical district, but most of his revenues came from what was then called the sticks. If he had a success on Broadway he thought of it only as a means of extracting money from the people beyond the two rivers. Any run of more than forty nights was enough to start him off. He would flood the provinces with propaganda whooping up the play as the greatest hit since " The Two Orphans," and in a few weeks he would follow that propaganda with a series of road companies, all of them outfitted with frantic press-agents and inflammatory billing. The press-agents he selected with care, mainly from among men who had had circus or bicycle-race experience, and the billing he wrote and designed himself, but to the casting of his companies he gave only casual attention, for it was his firm conviction that the provinces could not distinguish between geniuses and hams, and indeed were more apt to be pleased by hams than by geniuses. Whenever he was preparing a fresh assault upon them he would send in an order to a theatrical agency for so many head of bucks and so many head of wenches (this is how he always spoke of his hirelings) and in a little while rehearsals would be under way. But now and then, of course, he picked up a performer in some other manner — say through a letter of introduction from a theatre manager in Anniston, Ala., or Xenia, O., or a rare crash of his office trenches and pill-boxes.

This last happened in the case of the lady who was the culprit in the trial I am about to describe. She hailed from Nebraska, and had got her early training in a company playing "The Fatal Wedding" under canvas. When the rough travel and bad eating in the Western wilderness began to tell on her, she threw up her job and headed for New York. She had $375 in her stocking — the savings of two years of hard work —, and with this to sustain her she took a modest room in the forties and began a siege of the Broadway agents and managers. My friend's office was on her daily route, but it was a long while before he ever saw her, or even heard of her, for his office boy chased her out every time she showed up. This happened in all the other offices also, and she began to be uneasy, for her money was fast disappearing. One morning, after my friend's office boy — a gigantic lout who, in these days, would be called a gorilla — had been especially unkind to her, she burst into tears and dropped into a chair by the door to have her cry out. My friend, happening to come in at that moment, was struck by something or other in her appearance, and, being in a benignant mood, invited her into his private office to talk it over. The net result was not only a job, but also a love affair. In brief, my friend got mashed on her, and within a week she had moved from her meagre lodgings in the forties to a comfortable apartment in the fifties, and had a large outfit of new clothes, with a fur coat to top it off.

But though she was properly grateful, and told everyone she met (including me) that my friend was a prince and had a heart of gold, she still itched for the stimulation of the footlights, and in a little while she began agitating for a part in one of the road companies. My friend was not averse to giving her a chance, for he believed that she was probably bad enough, professionally, to please the provinces, but his feelings toward her were still very tender, and he was loath to be separated from her, maybe for four or five months. Presently he solved the problem by organizing a company to play one of his recent forty-night sensations in towns close to New York. The farthest it would get, according to the route laid out, would be Scranton, Pa., and during a large part of its tour, so he hoped, it would be playing at a dollar-top neighborhood theatre in Brooklyn. The girl was accordingly given the job of leading woman, and after two weeks in Pennsylvania and New Jersey, was safely anchored in Brooklyn for the run. This arrangement, for a while, was satisfactory to all parties at interest. The girl spent her days, save when there were matinées, on Manhattan Island, kept her clothes at the apartment in the fifties, and usually, though not always, returned there after the evening's performance in Brooklyn.

My friend, after the opening, never looked in on the company, for he was a very busy man, but he had a spy who visited it at intervals and reported on anything amiss — say, too much boozing by the company manager or some unusual butchery of the lines by the actors. One day, during the fourth or fifth week of the Brooklyn run, this spy came in with very unpleasant news. It was to the effect that the leading lady was carrying on injudiciously, not to say feloniously, with the leading man. They visited each other's dressing-rooms far more than they had any need for, and several times they had been detected in prolonged strangle-holds behind the back-drop. On the evenings following matinée days, when the girl, on the score of fatigue, remained in Brooklyn overnight, they disappeared together and were never seen by the other members of the company. The spy, as in duty bound, shadowed them on such an evening, and found them ducking into the leading man's quarters at a third-rate hotel. My friend was naturally upset by this report, but he had some suspicion of his spy, and so borrowed another one from a brother manager, and sent him to Brooklyn to check up. This second spy made the same report precisely. The girl was thereupon ordered to report in New York at 11 o'clock the next morning to stand her trial.

I was not, of course, present at this proceeding, but my friend described it to me at great length the next time I was in New York, and I am sure that he gave me a reasonably accurate account of it, for he was a truthful fellow, despite his business, and he had a special confidence in and kindness for me, for I was the only dramatic reviewer in America, save only Stuffy Davis of the New York *Globe*, who had never tried to sell him a play. He said that the girl appeared at his office promptly, and declined his offer to let her have counsel. Instead, she made a complete confession, instantly and without urging, and in it went much further than either of the spies had alleged. It was quite true, she said, that she and the leading man were carrying on as alleged. It had begun, in fact, before the end of the first week in Brooklyn, and it was still in progress. Moreover, she refused flatly to make any promise of an abatement, either then or thereafter, though she admitted freely that her conduct was clearly immoral.

My friend told me that this confession not only shocked him, but also greatly astonished him. He had, of course, heard " Rigoletto " and hence knew that women were mobile, but here, it seemed to him, mobility had quite run amuck. The insult to his vanity he could bear, for he was a philosopher, but the puzzle that went with it really racked him. Why on earth should a girl apparently sane engage in any such degrading and irrational malpractises with an obscure and ignominious actor, a cheap clown in a No. 5 road company, a mere ham? Why should she turn from a salient and even (in her world) distinguished man and take up with so grotesque a nonentity? My friend, who had no false modesty, told me that he put the question to her plainly. On the one side, he reminded her, was himself — a fellow of large means and generous impulses, a figure of consequence on Broadway, her tried friend and benefactor, and last but not least, a man who wore expensive and well-cut clothes and was commonly conceded to be of imposing presence. On the other was that wretched ham — a poor fish who would never get beyond the lowest rounds of his profession and was doomed to penury all his life long; moreover, a grotesque figure in his cheap and flashy garments, with a hair-cut that no he-man would tolerate, a ring on his finger set with a bogus diamond, a preposterous walking-stick, and a complexion that inevitably suggested (when his make-up was washed off) both inebriety and malnutrition. What had become of the boasted sagacity of the female sex? How could any woman abandon and betray so upstanding and admirable a man as my friend and make off with that hideous caricature?

She had, it appeared, an answer ready. She had pleaded guilty, but nevertheless she was not without a defense. She did not deny the tremendous disparity between my friend and the actor. On the contrary, she admitted it freely, and even added that it was greater than had been represented. "I am here to tell you honestly," she said to my friend, "that you are the most elegant man I have ever met. No one could be more attractive to a sensible woman. You are rich, generous, smart, celebrated and handsome. I love to hear you talk, and I even like to see you eat. You have treated me better than a queen. When I put you beside that ham it really makes me laugh: compared to you he is a rat beside a hippopotamus. But" — and she paused a bit, as an actress would, to drive the point home — "but you are here in New York, rolling in your glory — and I am out there in the wilds of Brooklyn, alone and forlorn, trying to get that terrible play over to great gangs of smelly idiots.

"Have you ever tried to figure out what that means to a refined woman? Can you imagine yourself making up in a damp, drafty dressing-room night after night, and then going out on that creaky stage and speaking the same lines over and over again to those blockheads? No; I thought not. But that is what I have to do, and, believe me, it is no easy job. Sometimes I make such a mess of my performance that I burst into tears at every exit. Well, every time I do that there is that ham standing in the wings. He comes up to me, puts his arms around me, and says 'You are wonderful tonight, darling! I watched you fascinated. You really moved me.' Do I swallow it? Naturally not. I know that I have been lousy,[1] but there he is waiting for me, to tell me that I haven't. Let me say to you that such words are music to the ear of a woman. They fetch us every time. Maybe, if it had been anywhere else but Brooklyn I might have pulled myself together and given that ham a clout over the ear, but the first time he tried me it was pouring down rain outside and the audience smelled like a cat-show, and so I fell for it. After that he had me. I knew it was crazy, but I simply couldn't resist. He never had anything to say about himself: it was always *me, me, me*. He had me acting rings around Nazimova. He got me so that when I looked in my dressing-room mirror I saw Lillian Russell. So that is my story, and you can take it or leave it."

My friend told me that it took him no more than a minute to reach his decision; he had formulated it, in fact, before the girl finished her speech. As friend, as philanthropist, as man, he was injured, outraged — but as psychologist he was hooked and landed. What answer, indeed, could he make to the

1 This term was still a novelty in 1912, even on Broadway. It came in toward the end of 1911.

girl's argument? He could think of none whatsoever. His verdict simply had to be self-defense, and his sentence was so mild that it amounted to a parole: he bade her return to Brooklyn and try to avoid the ham as much as possible. He even let her keep the apartment in the fifties, though in view of the circumstances he had his own belongings moved out by his spy the next morning.

XI

A ROMAN HOLIDAY

[*1914*]

Most of my traveling, whether by land or by sea, has been done on business, and in consequence there has usually been a good deal more hard labor in it than *dolce far niente*. For twenty years on end I had jobs as a magazine editor in New York but kept my home in Baltimore, which meant that I had to make the round trip every couple of weeks, and sometimes oftener. These journeys, if I had been able to look out of the train windows, would have made me minutely familiar with all the scenery along the two hundred miles, but as it was I always had to keep my nose buried in manuscripts, and seldom saw anything save an occasional sash-weight factory or cow, glimpsed vaguely out of the corner of my eye. When this servitude ended, at the beginning of 1934, I employed a statistician to figure out how many words I had read during the twenty years, but when his report came in it was so full of plus and minus signs and unintelligible gabble about skew distributions and coefficients of correlation that I threw it away in disgust, and fell back on my own bare-hand guess, which was 50,000,000 words. My longer journeys, before, during and after the same time, were made principally for newspapers, and save when I contrived to get myself lost were even worse, for they were punctuated day and night by telegrams from managing editors reading " Where is your second follow lead? ", " Please call in between 11.30 p.m. and 11.40 Eastern Standard Daylight Time," or " Your story differs from the A.P. in the following particulars. . . . Please confirm or correct." All the reporters that I traveled with got the same telegrams, and not infrequently, when I received an especially outrageous one, I would change the address on it and pass it to one of my colleagues. Unhappily, the other boys and gals resorted to the same trick, with the effect that on a bad night I was bombarded with remonstrances from managing editors stretching from San Diego to Boston. No one, of course, save a greenhorn or a lunatic ever answered such messages, but nevertheless they were irritating, and after reading them for a couple of weeks I was almost in a mood for the plunge into delirium tremens that they had been accusing me of, usually only covertly but sometimes in plain English, all the while.

But there were a number of times when I threw

off such chains, and traveled for the pure deviltry of it, and it is such trips that I always remember most vividly when I am laid up with rheumatism and try to forget it in memories of my dead life. Of all those unofficial or illicit journeys, the one that I recall with the most pleasure is a jaunt in reverse along the route of the classical Grand Tour of Europe, made in the Spring of 1914 in the company of two Baltimore friends, W. Edwin Moffett and A. H. McDannald, the latter my companion on a previous pilgrimage, already mentioned in Chapter IX. Moffett is now a bull-fiddle virtuoso of such wizardry that I have actually seen and heard a symphony concert audience rise up and cheer him, and McDannald has gone so far in learning that he is the editor-in-chief of an encyclopedia, but in 1914 they were both simple fellows out for a gaudy time, as I was myself, and we unquestionably had it in Italy, Switzerland, Germany and France, not to mention the Atlantic Ocean and the Mediterranean Sea. We made the eastward ocean trip in a second-string Cunarder called the *Laconia*, one of the first of the so-called tour-ships. It was slow but very comfortable, and when we left New York we looked forward to nine lazy days to Gibraltar. We planned to spend them in the smokeroom, for all three of us believed that the glare of the sun on deck was deleterious, and had tried to put away temptation by making a pact to hire no deck-chairs. This, of course, got the deck-stewards down on us, but the bar-stewards were very polite and assiduous, and it was generally understood before we reached Nantucket light that one of the best corners in the smokeroom was ours. But our dream of crossing the ocean in peace and comfort did not last much longer, for on the first day out the usual pests got together to form the usual committees, and thereafter we were beset day and night by women selling tickets to concerts, chances on raffles, or knitted neckties made by inmates of the Sailors' Orphans' Home at Liverpool, or worse still, trying to wheedle us into going to mask balls, joining in folk-song festivals, or making speeches. Moffett put off these harpies for a few days by pointing to his right ear and bellowing "Deef! Deef!" and Mac pretended that I was a homicidal maniac and he my keeper, but the gals quickly got on to these subterfuges, and settled down in brutal earnest to fetch us.

We were, however, tough guys in those days, and as incredible as it may seem we actually came into sight of the coast of Portugal without going to a single dance, concert, raffle, spelling-bee, debate, sing-song or mass-meeting, and without contributing a single nickel to any home for decrepit sailors, or their (probably illegitimate) offspring, or their deserted wives, or their sorrowing old fathers and mothers, from the Orkney islands to Capetown. Every time the smokeroom stewards saw us throw off another solicitor they set up the drinks on the house, for, as they told us, it was unprecedented for a male passenger in the Cunard to escape his inevitable doom for such a stretch of time. Many, of course, held out for a day or two, and a few extraordinarily recalcitrant curmudgeons stood it for three days, or even four, but never since the *Britannia* sailed from Liverpool on July 4, 1840 had anyone ever survived so long as a week. This happy state of affairs prevailed until the night before we made Gibraltar, and we attained to such eminence aboard that not a few other passengers, escaping momentarily from whatever horror was afoot, came to the smokeroom door to gape at us and admire us. But after dinner that evening the massed committees of the ship's company combined to assault and rout us, and after an all-too-brief and far from glorious struggle we were had.

I need not add, I hope, that it was not argument that took us, nor anything properly describable as an appeal to our better nature: it was simply the use of female pulchritude, and in the rawest and most unsportsmanlike fashion. Hitherto all the ladies who had tackled us had been mature and even more or less overripe damsels of the sort who naturally take to good works, whether on land or sea. The worst of them came close to looking like members of the W.C.T.U., and even the best, when they were not plainly retired opera singers or cashiered stock-company actresses, carried about them a faint, sickening suggestion of Christian endeavor. But now all that orthodox but puerile technic was out of the window, and the master-minds of the committees, laying their heads together, were trying us with a new and far sharper excalibur. In brief, they rounded up the three rosiest, sweetest, triggest, archest, sauciest and all-round charmingest cuties in the ship, and set them on us as a pot-hunter might turn a pack of bloodhounds upon a poor fieldmouse. We had never seen these cuties before, for they had spent all their time dancing in the social hall, and our own station, as I have said, had been in the smokeroom, but now, as they bore down upon us with pretty giggles, we got a massive eyeful, and in ten seconds we were undone. Nor did we recover when they began unloading the selling-talk that the committeemen had prepared for them. What they wanted us to do, they explained ever so alluringly, was to squire them to a mock wedding that was presently to be staged in the dining-room, which had been cleared for the occasion. They were to appear at this mock wedding in the character of bridesmaids, and we were to be ushers. No rehearsal, they assured us, would be necessary. So far as our own participation was concerned, it would be a wedding like any other, and if occasional prompting turned out to be necessary they would supply it, at the same time hanging on to our arms. All the speaking parts were in other hands. *Allons*, comrades, the audience waits! Moffett, with a faint blush for the smokeroom stewards who glared reproachfully from behind their bar, offered his arm to a blonde who looked like Lillian Russell at the age of seventeen, Mac grabbed a little brunette who seemed to be of mixed Russian, French, Spanish, Algonquin and angel blood, and I was left with a red-haired girl so lovely that when I looked at her I saw only an explosion of rubies and amethysts.

Thus we were bagged, and thus we marched ignominiously to the dining-room, each hanging on to his Delilah. A large company of poor fish was already assembled, and the chief bore of the ship, a loud, officious, Rotarian-sort of fellow, was planted under an arch of British flags in the low comedy rôle of the officiating clergyman. Presently the ship's bugler blew five or six measures of the "Lohengrin" wedding march, the bride and groom marched in from the pantry, the best man and chief bridesmaid fell in behind them, and Moffett, Mac and I, with our trio of palpitating pretties, took up the rear. Of the bride I can only recall that she was a fair specimen of run-of-the-mine goods, and of the bridegroom only that he looked considerably alarmed. Later on I heard that the bride actually had her eye on him, and that they became engaged while visiting the grave of Percy Bysshe Shelley at Rome. But on that point I have only rumor, and moreover, it is irrelevant. What I remember most clearly, and indeed with a sort of dizzy dazzle, is the marriage service that the Rotarian began to read. It opened as follows:

Dearly beloved, we are gathered here together in the face of this company to join together this man and woman in asceptic matrimony, which is commended by Mendel, Ehrlich, Metchnikoff and others to be honorable among men, and therefore is not to be entered into inadvisedly or carelessly, or without due surgical precautions, but reverently, cleanly, sterilely, soberly, scientifically, and with the nearest practicable approach to chemical purity.

And so on, and so on. The audience, at first, was astonished into silence, but in a little while a few women began to titter, and soon there were snorts all over the room. The three cuties took it very merrily, and mine gave me more than one dig in the ribs with her incomparable elbow. Meanwhile, the Rotarian boomed on in roaring tones, calling upon the bridegroom to say so plainly if he were suffering from any "lesion, infection, malaise, congenital defect, hereditary taint or other impediment," and finally commanding him to produce medical certificates or forever hold his peace. At this, the bridegroom took a long envelope from his inside pocket and handed it to the Rotarian, who broke its seal in a very ceremonious manner, withdrew a paper fluttering a red ribbon, and proceeded to read from it as follows:

We, and each of us, having subjected the bearer to a rigid clinical and laboratory examination, do hereby certify that, to the best of our knowledge and belief, he is free from all disease, taint, defect, deformity or hereditary blemish. Temperature *per ora:* 98.6. Pulse: 76, strong. Respiration: 28.5. Wassermann: minus two. Phthalein: first hour, 46 per cent; second hour, 21 per cent. White blood corpuscle count: 8,925. Free gastric hydrochloric acid: 11.5 per cent. No stasis. No lactic acid.

By this time the dining-room was in an uproar, and the three cuties seemed to be on the point of busting with laughter. I was somewhat amused myself, and, in secret, delighted, but I was even more astounded, for *I had written that wedding service myself*. Yea, I had not only written it, but printed it, to wit, in the *Smart Set* for October 1913, pp. 63 *ff*.[1] Thus I listened to the Rotarian's somewhat sketchy and ruffianly version of it with all the fascination that enthralls any dramatic author when he sees his own play on the stage, and while the thing was going on I gave scarcely a thought to the throbbing virgin at my side. Nor did Mac pay any attention to his delectable brunette, for he had read the piece in the magazine and knew that I had written it. When the show was over, to great salvos of huzzahs at the end, the three cuties deserted us for their regular platoons of beaux, and we resumed our pews in the smokeroom. It may be that the Rotarian, in one of his innumerable bulletins and speeches to his suffering fellow-passengers, had given proper credit to the author, but if so we

1 It was entitled A Eugenic Wedding and was signed Owen Hatteras, a *nom de plume* I used in those days whenever my monthly contributions to the *Smart Set* were so numerous that they could not all be published under my own name. With the title changed to Asepsis: A Deduction in *Scherzo* Form, it was reprinted in my Book of Burlesques; New York, 1916.

heard nothing of it, and Mac, who was a *legum baccalaureus* of the University of Virginia and full of lingering Confederate war-lust, was all for suing him in the courts for infringement of copyright. This seemed a bad idea to me, for the copyright had been taken out, not in my name, but in that of the *Smart Set*, and anything we recovered from the Rotarian would go to John Adams Thayer, then the proprietor of the magazine. Inasmuch as Thayer was already very well heeled, I could see no sense in engorging him further, but Mac insisted that important principles were at stake, and also conjured up a number of interesting questions of law. Could we sue the Rotarian in Gibraltar, where we were due to land the next morning, or would we have to wait until we got back to New York? Furthermore, wasn't the Cunard Steamship Company responsible, as *particeps criminis*, and if so couldn't we proceed against it in admiralty, libel the *Laconia*, hang up the tour, and expose the ship to hundreds of claims for damages to the other passengers? Mac had no law-books with him, and in fact had not looked into one since he took his degree in 1898, but he kept on laboring the matter until the smokeroom stewards turned out the lights on us at 3 a.m. and we had to go to bed. The next morning, after we had landed on the Rock and were getting down *Humpen* of bicarbonate of soda in its only drug-store, he resumed the subject, but as the bicarbonate began to open the pores of his mind he forgot it, and after that I heard no more from him about it. Whether or not the Rotarian really lifted my play without credit I do not know to this day. If he did, then I forgive him belatedly and wish him good luck in his chosen career, whatever it may be.

A few days later the *Laconia* reached Naples and we went ashore through the barrage of bumboats, broken-down steam-launches and other such crazy craft that once made a riot of that lovely port. The depth of water at the docks was then insufficient to float an ocean steamer, and passengers had to be ferried in row-boats. These row-boats were operated by members of the Black Hand, and they hated one another almost as much as they hated humanity in general. Thus getting to land was a more or less hazardous business, for the instant a passenger appeared at the gangway all the Black Handers for a block around began to fight for his business. Nor was the battle over when one of them got him, for the rest proceeded to ram the victorious boat, and to prod both its operator and its passenger with their oars. It was very uncommon for a passenger to get ashore without being doused, and not infrequently he lost his baggage. On the quay he went through another similar mauling, for the customs-house red-caps, all of them gorillas brought in from the penitentiaries of Sicily, fought for him just as the boatmen had fought for him. It is a literal fact that it took Ed, Mac and me two hours to get through the customs, though we had nothing to declare and the actual officials were very polite. All the delay was caused by our porters, who had to fight for us from the moment they collared us until they finally landed us on the street. This fighting, of course, was not done in silence. The screaming and howling, in fact, were even worse than the jostling, and by the time the three of us got to our hotel in the Via Caracciolo we were pretty well worn out.

This, of course, was before the days of Mussolini, and Italy was still innocent of efficiency engineering. Exactly twenty years later, in 1934, I returned to Naples, again by sea. I was aboard a German liner of at least twice the tonnage of the *Laconia*, but it tied up at a dock with the greatest ease and even elegance. Looking ashore, I could see nothing of the frantic Black Handers of 1914. At the far end of the dock a long row of taxicabs was lined up, and between them and the ship stood four or five men in uniform. Whenever a passenger went ashore one of these functionaries approached him politely, asked him if he required a taxi, whistled for one if he said yes, and then put him aboard it with a deep bow. There was no more uproar than you will hear in the middle of the Mojave Desert, and not the slightest sign of excitement. Going ashore for a little walk, I seemed to be in a city that had died and been embalmed. Where were the sellers of dirty postcards that had swarmed over Ed,

Mac and me in 1914? Where were the loud and urgent guides to Pompeii, to the art galleries, to the bawdy-houses? Where were the hawkers plastered with lottery-tickets? Where was all the old-time hullabaloo? Alas, it had gone with the wind, and a Fascist calm prevailed. After walking for a while I came to a little square, and there, across the grass, I saw an evil-looking youth who took me back twenty years. He saw me too, and began to approach me in a stealthy, furtive way, pausing anon to glance back over his shoulder. If any human being ever had seller of dirty postcards written on his face it was that unappetizing young wop, and I halted to give him a chance to make his sales approach. I was not, of course, in the market for his wares, but I yearned to hear him for old time's sake. But when he was not more than fifteen feet from me he stopped suddenly, stared over my shoulder like a pointer become aware of a quail, turned white with an unearthly greenish cast, and then made off to starboard with long, nervous, skulking strides, and vanished into the shadows of an alley. As he disappeared I about-faced to find out what had alarmed him. Half a block away I saw a perfect simulacrum of Benito Himself — an obvious plain-clothes man in the Fascist béret, his legs planted firmly, his arms folded in authoritative challenge, an imitation of the Mussolini frown upon his face. Such were the hazards of an innocent and industrious dirty-postcard vendor under the New Order in Italy. Such was life in sterilized and dephlogisticated Naples, once so gay with iniquities and stinks. Such, I reflected sadly, was human progress.

But in 1914 Naples was still as free and natural as it had been in the days when its bristling walls scared off Hannibal. Its main streets had not been swept since the Sixteenth Century, and in many of its alleys there was an accumulation of garbage going back to Roman times. Ed, Mac and I had a grand time exploring its marvels and devouring its garlicky and excellent victuals. One day we went out to Capri and got lost among its vineyards, and another day we hoofed the ruins of Pompeii and were introduced by a friendly guide to an antique factory adjacent, where we saw the workmen turning out Roman bronzes by the gross, all plainly marked 200 B.C., to reassure tourists. At night we would resort to the Galleria Umberto and listen to the singing contests going on there all the time. We had two large rooms at our hotel, with a magnificent bathroom adjoining, including a shower. On the morning after our arrival I arose before the others, and went to this bathroom to take a bath. First I soaped myself from head to foot and then I got under the shower and turned the handle. But no water came out. Seeing a small stool in a corner, I mounted it to investigate, but I could not solve the mystery, and soon the soap got into my eyes and blinded me, and I had to call for help. Mac responded by beating on all the pipes with the heel of one of his shoes, but the more practical Ed went to the telephone and called up the office. The clerk below, it appeared, could not understand English, and Ed's Italian was far from perfect. While I tried to mop off the soap with a towel ten feet long I could hear him roaring into the 'phone: "Da wat' no come in da pipe! Da dam machina no worka! Senda da chief engineer dam quicka!"

In a few minutes there was a rap at the door, and Mac admitted a chambermaid. She was armed with a broom, a bucket, a mop and various other apparatus, and turned out, fortunately, to have a a few words of German, so I soon explained to her, clad in that mainsail of a towel, what was wrong. She was an efficient woman, as efficiency ran in Italy in those days, and instantly fell to work. First, she turned on the water full tilt — but it still refused to flow. Then she put the stool into the tub, mounted it, withdrew a large hairpin from her hair, and proceeded to investigate the sprinkler. The first hole she tackled turned out to be solid with rust, but she managed by hard gouging to coax a drop of water out of it. Encouraged, she turned to a hole in the center of the sprinkler, and gave it a sudden and powerful jab. There was a large scab of rust inside, apparently covering half a dozen holes. When this scab gave way it gave way all over, and as a result she got a rush of water squarely in the eye, and went over backward, yelling blue murder. The scene followed the most austere lines of classical farce; in fact, it was worthy of Billy Watson's Beef Trust. Ed, Mac and I whooped and roared in our vulgar mirth, but when the lady became bellicose we threw her out, and I resumed my bath. When we shoved off for Rome the hotel's bill showed an item of two lire for repairing the shower, but Mac threatened suit and we got away without paying it.

We arrived in Rome late at night, and after taking a walk and a couple of drinks rolled into the hay. The next morning we were up bright and early, and on our way to St. Peter's. There we put in two or three hours admiring its wonders, especially the immense *pissoir* on the roof — the largest in Europe —, and by noon we found ourselves in the alley between the cathedral and the Vatican, thumbing through postcards at a stand there set up. While we were so engaged an American we had met on the ship strolled up, and the four of us decided to lunch together. But before we could set off for an eating-house we noticed a group of people gathered about a priest a little farther up the alley, with the priest haranguing them violently. It seemed worth looking into, so we approached the group and I noted that the priest was talking German. From his remarks it quickly appeared that his customers were pious pilgrims from Vienna, that they had been forty-eight hours in day-coaches on the way — I could well believe it by their smell —, that they had an appointment to be received by the Pope, that the time set was only a few minutes hence, and that their pastor was giving them a last-minute refresher course in Vatican etiquette. Over and over again he explained to them the stage management of a papal audience, and cautioned them to behave in a seemly and Christian manner. They would be lined up on their knees, he said, and His Holiness would walk down the line, blessing them as he went and offering them his ring to kiss. Under no circumstances were they to attempt to kiss his hand, but only the ring. "Nicht die Hand!" he kept on repeating. "Küsst den Ring!" Nor did he stop with this brief, almost military order: he also went into the considerations lying behind it. What a scandal it would be, he said, if the illustrious Pope of Rome, the spiritual father of the whole universe, were exposed in his own almost sacred person to the lewd osculation of the vulgar! What an insult to His Holiness, and what a source of obscene joy to the vast hordes of infidels! His ring was provided as a means of warding off any such calamity. It, and not his hand, was to be kissed. "Nicht die Hand, Kinder! Küsst den Ring!"

So saying, he signaled the pilgrims to follow him. As they moved over toward a door making into the Vatican I looked at Mac, Mac looked at Ed, Ed looked at the stranger from the *Laconia*, and the stranger looked at me. Why not, indeed? The group was large enough for us to be lost in it, and the pilgrims seemed to be of very low mental visibility. As for the priest, he was marching ahead of them, with his back to them and us. We therefore ducked among them, and in a minute we were marching down one of the long corridors of the Vatican, headed for the audience chamber. I expected to see a large hall elegantly turned out, with maybe a couple of pictures by Raphael or Leonardo on its walls, but the priest actually led us into a series of modest rooms that looked like parlors in a bourgeois home. They were arranged *en suite*, and the Pope, I gathered, would traverse them one after another. The priest was in the room nearest His Holiness's entrance, but when he issued a command that we fall on our knees it was relayed down the line, and we all obeyed. Mac kneeled to my left and Ed to my right and beyond Ed was the stranger. We waited patiently, but in some uneasiness. What if we were detected? Would the Swiss guards who stood at every door simply throw us out, or would it be a matter for the police? We had not long to suffer, for in a minute there was a murmur in the room beyond us and in another minute the Pope was passing before us, holding out his ring to be kissed.

He was Pius X, born Sarto, already an ancient man and beginning to break up. From the floor where we kneeled he looked tall, but I doubt that he was so in fact. His skin was of a startling whiteness, and he stooped from the effects of a large swelling at the back of his neck — not, of course, a goitre, but of the same general dimensions and aspect. As he came into our room, preceded by a chamberlain and followed by two guards, an ormolu clock on the marble mantelpiece struck twelve. He moved slowly and with effort, and appeared to be almost unaware of his visitors, though he held out his hand for the kissing of his ring, and smiled wanly. Save for the whispered words of his blessing he said nothing, and neither did any of the pilgrims. He had been Pope, by now, for eleven years, and was close to eighty years old. A man of deep piety and simple tastes, he had resisted, back in 1880, an effort to make him Bishop of Treviso, but a few years later he had been caught by the cogs of the Roman escalator and by 1893 he was the Cardinal Patriarch of Venice and ten years later he was Pope. His reign, alas, had not been any too peaceful: there had been struggles with France, turmoils among the Italian bishops, and all sorts of vexatious disputes — about the powers and jurisdictions of the Papal courts, the text of canon law, the nomination of bishops, the reform of the breviary and of church music, and so on without ceasing. He looked immensely old as he passed so slowly before us, and pretty well worn out. But he walked without help, and in less than two minutes he was gone. This was in May, 1914. Two months later a shot was fired at Sarajevo in faraway Bosnia, and on August 2 World War I began. His Holiness survived that blasting of all his hopes of peace on earth by less than three weeks. On August 20 he was dead.

Once he vanished, Mac, Ed, the stranger and I made tracks out of the room, for we feared that the priest might come back and discover us. Without anyone to guide us, we got lost at once, and were presently astonished to find ourselves in the Sistine Chapel. It was quite empty, and we hid there for ten minutes — long enough to throw off the scent. Then we tried the first long corridor that offered, and at its end found a door which took us out into the glare of noontime Rome. A horse-hack was waiting nearby, and in it we rode grandly to our hotel. There was a large assemblage of *Laconia* passengers in the dining-room, and some of them asked us where we had been. When we replied that we had been undergoing the honor of an audience with the Pope there were sniffs of incredulity, and mingled with that incredulity there was not a little hostility. Some of those other passengers were pious Catholics come to Rome for the express purpose of paying their respects to His Holiness, but when they had gone to the American College that morning to apply for an audience they had been told that it would involve a great many onerous formalities and probably a long wait. So many applications were piled up, in fact, that the best the clergy at the college could promise, even to a ninth-degree Knight of Columbus and his lady, was a possible look-in some time in July. Actual bishops, it appeared, were hanging about for weeks before their numbers turned up. Moreover, all the lay applicants were warned that their appointments, if, when and as obtained at all, would be for designated weeks, not for specific days, and that they might have to stand by from end to end of those weeks, the men in boiled shirts and tail coats and the ladies in black gowns with long sleeves. If, at the moment of their summons, they were not so arrayed, they would miss their turns, and maybe have to wait three months before they were called again.

All of this, naturally enough, had filled the pilgrims with unpleasant sentiments, and they were in no mood to listen with any appreciation to the tale of our own exploit. It was already very hot in Rome, and they could well imagine what it would be like in July or August to sit in unventilated hotel rooms for a week on end, clad in boiled shirts and long sleeves. At the start, they eased their minds by denouncing us as liars of unparalleled effrontery, but as we added various details in support of our narrative, they had to admit that we were probably telling something more or less resembling the truth, and thereupon they took refuge in the theory that our uninvited visit was not only an insult to the Pope, but also a carnal and blasphemous attack upon Holy Church itself, and upon the True Faith that it inculcated. The Knights of Columbus present were all too old and bulky to hope to beat us up, but they talked darkly of employing Black Handers for the purpose, and even hinted that they knew a Jesuit who could supply the Black Handers. We replied primly that there was a lawyer in our outfit, and that if any such threats were carried out he would know how to launch the secular law upon all persons responsible. This seemed to daunt the knights, who had a high reverence for the police of all nations, and they gradually subsided into mutterings about the impertinence of Protestants, and, even worse, of infidels, and the need of laws barring them from the capital of Christendom. All we could reply to that was that Teddy Roosevelt and William Jennings Bryan were both Protestants, and that Thomas Jefferson had been an infidel. It was a somewhat feeble argument, and we did not press it. In consequence, the debate gradually petered out, and when we left at last the knights and their ladies had gone back to discussing the discomforts of boiled shirts and long sleeves in hot weather.

Having now seen both St. Peter's and the Vatican and enjoyed the distinction — whether honorable or infamous — of having been received by the Pope in private audience, we decided that we had given enough time to Rome and its environs, and the next day we set out for Munich by the Brenner Express. We had an instructive and somewhat noisy time in that beautiful city, but for the purposes of the present narrative what we saw, heard and did during our visit is neither here nor there.

XII

WINTER VOYAGE

[*1916*]

In the closing days of 1916, having been hired by a newspaper to investigate the war raging in Europe, I sailed from New York in a Danish ship, and seventeen days later found myself in Copenhagen. It was a slow trip, even for war time, but my recollections of it do not have to do with its duration, but with two relatively minor details: (*a*) the excessively mixed and belligerent nature of the ship's company, and (*b*) the stupendous eating and drinking that went on aboard. Nearly every nationality that I had heard of up to that time was represented among the passengers, and each *bloc* hated and reviled all the others. It did not surprise me, of course, to find the Germans and French on somewhat distant terms, or the Poles and Austrians, but I was certainly amazed when it turned out that the Danes, Norwegians, Swedes and Finns were bitter enemies, each to the other three, that the only Scotsman refused to speak to the Englishmen, and that the French actually joined the Germans in contemning and excoriating the Italians.

At meals I sat at the doctor's table, with a Russian general in the place of honor at the other end. This general, who wore stupendous Hindenburg mustaches, glared at his trough-fellows through breakfast, lunch and dinner, and refused either to speak to them or to answer them when they spoke to him. The theory arose that he probably knew no language save Russian, so a Czech who spoke it was brought up from the second cabin to tackle him. The general, for perhaps five minutes, took no notice whatever, but the Czech was a persistent fellow, and finally dredged a single sentence out of those fearful mustaches. He reported that it was a profane declaration, *in Russian,* that the general could not speak Russian. How he talked to his adjutant, who sat beside him, I do not know, for they exchanged only grunts at meals, and between meals they disappeared.

All during those intervals, I suppose, the general slept in his cabin, for it is hard to imagine anyone keeping awake after the gargantuan feeds he got down. Certainly they never ran to less than 45,000 calories apiece, not counting bread, butter and the sugar in the coffee. Well do I recall his breakfast on the first day out, for it was a rough morning, and most of the other passengers at our table confined themselves to toast and tea. But not the general. He began with three oranges *au naturel*, followed them with a large plate of oatmeal swimming in cream, topped it with a double order of ham and eggs, and then proceeded to run through all the Danish delicacies on the table — six or eight kinds of smoked fish, as many of sausage, a bowl of pickled pigs' ears, another of spiced lambs' tongues, a large slab of Gjedser cheese, and five or six slices of toasted rye-bread spread with red caviare. To wash down this mammoth *frokost* he drank four cups of coffee and two of tea. When he finished at last a couple of waiters rushed up to help him to his feet, but he shook them off, arose with the dignity of Neptune emerging from the sea, and stalked away in his best parade-ground manner. His adjutant, following at a respectful six paces, wobbled precariously, for the ship was doing a forty-degree roll, but the general was still as perpendicular as a meridian of longitude when he disappeared down the corridor to his quarters.

By lunchtime the weather had moderated considerably, and all hands at the table were ready for earnest eating, but the general was in full form by now and managed to grab so much of everything that there was little left for the rest of us. He was aided in this enterprise by the fact that the rules of the Danish merchant marine in those days — and, for all I know, the constitution of Denmark — ordained that everything after the soup should be brought to the table on large platters and passed round. This passing round, of course, should have started with the ship's doctor at the head of the table — an old man in a long beard, and himself, as it soon appeared, no contemptible glutton — but the waiters had to come in through a door that was just behind the general's chair, and he thus got first whack at them — no doubt illegally, but none the less effectively, for he grabbed their arms if they tried to pass him. The pièce de résistance at that first lunch was a pair of gigantic cabbages stuffed with sausage meat and decorated with potato balls, beets and turnips cut into fancy designs, and hard-boiled eggs. The general nabbed the larger of the two cabbages, and had got half of it down before the other one could be carved by the doctor and served to the remaining fourteen men at the table. The doctor, incensed, instructed the waiters to make a detour around the general thereafter, but he turned out to have a reach like a gorilla, and when one of them presently staggered in with a huge plate of spare ribs and sauerkraut he had nailed two-thirds of the spare ribs and nearly all the sauerkraut before you could say Jack Robinson. And so with every other dish that followed — maybe six or eight in all, for the Danes fed their customers as if fattening them for slaughter. But it was not until the end of lunch that the general let go the last link of his virtuosity. By that time, though we had got only his meagre leavings, we were all pretty well filled, and hence hardly fit to do justice to the gigantic board of Danish pastry that ended the meal. But not the general. There were twelve separate and distinct kinds of pastry on it — and he grabbed two of each. When, having got them down, he began work on six cups of coffee, his mustaches glittered like a Christmas tree with the accumulated marmalade, powdered sugar and whipped cream.

The ship's doctor, during the two or three days following, tried various schemes to curb and baffle the old boy, but they all failed, and the only remedy remaining was to order double rations for the table. This was done, and an extra waiter was added to help rassle them, but the general improved as the service improved, and at the end of the first week the double rations had to be lifted to treble. Rather curiously, we never saw him take a drink of anything alcoholic. For a couple of days after this abstemiousness was remarked a theory floated about that he was off the stuff in compliment to King George V of England, who had gone on the water-wagon at the beginning of the war, but in the end most of the other men at the table chose to believe rather that he knocked off a quart or so of vodka before every meal, in the quiet of his quarters. We discussed him constantly despite his presence, for it was assumed as a matter of course that he knew no English, which was the common language of the table. Because of his mustaches the boys gave him the name of the Walrus. He never took any notice of these debates about him, nor did he show any resentment when all hands downed tools to watch him snare a whole leg of veal, or wolf another double dozen of Danish pastries. These pastries changed at every meal: it was the boast of the line that the same one was never served twice. The Walrus ate two of each variety at lunch and three at dinner. At the end of the long voyage, as we were all shivering in the customs shed at Copenhagen, he addressed a fellow passenger for the first time — and in excellent English. "I knew," he said, "that you called me the Walrus, but I didn't give a damn." Then he made off in the car of the Russian minister to Denmark, and was seen no more.

His avoidance of alcohol would have made him a marked man on that ship, even if he had confined himself to ordinary eating, for he was the only teetotaler, whether actual or apparent, among the passengers. The rest guzzled day and night, full of a resigned belief that a German submarine might fetch them all at any minute. We were at sea on New Year's Eve, somewhere off the coast of Greenland. It was too cold to go on deck, so the whole ship's company gathered in the smokeroom in the early afternoon, and gradually worked up a party of the very highest amperage. It appeared that it was the custom of the line for the ship's band, on such gala occasions, to play the national airs of all the countries represented among the passengers, but this time the captain forbade it, for he feared riots. Along toward midnight one of the Americans aboard played a joke on the band (and the captain) by digging up a *potpourri* of harmless German folk-songs (it began with " O Tannenbaum ") and asking the leader to put it on. The leader, who was also the bull fiddler, was so far gone in liquor by now that he could hardly stand up to his instrument, so he agreed amiably and at once plunged into the music. He either did not know, or had forgotten in his cups, that it ended with " Die Wacht am Rhein." Before he could pull up he was down to " Lieb' Vaterland, magst ruhig sein," and a Class A rough-house was in the making.

The Germans aboard (they were on their way home from Mexico and points South under a sort of flag of truce) were all either septuagenarians or cripples, but they leaped to their feet as one man, and began to *hoch* and howl in loud, exultant tones. This, of course, brought forth hoots and hisses from the English, Scotch, Canadians, French, Belgians, Russians, Japs, Italians and Rumanians, with encouragement from most of the Americans, Scandinavians, Hollanders and Latin Americans. When the first beer glass smashed a window the waiters and musicians took to flight, and in half a minute the master-at-arms was on the job with a squad of sailors, and on his heels came the captain. " Die Wacht am Rhein " having been played, the captain now had to admit that, in common equity, all the other national anthems should be played also, and when the musicians were rounded up and brought back it was solemnly done, with the master-at-arms and his goons mounting guard. At the end of the ceremonial two Swedes sitting in a corner rose up to protest that the anthem of Sweden had been forgotten. It was then that the enmity between the various Scandinavian nations became most painfully apparent, for the Danish leader of the band, half sober after his scare, replied sneeringly that Sweden *had* no anthem. The Norwegians and Danes cheered this insult, whereupon the two Swedes climbed up on their table and announced that they would *sing* their anthem, band or no band. This they did in indifferent voices, while the master-at-arms and his men kept order with drawn clubs and knives.

The party lasted for three days and nights; in fact, it was still going on, at least in spots, when we were hauled into Kirkwall and the English came out to search the ship and investigate its passengers. During this business, which went on intermittently for two days and ended with a dozen passengers being taken off for internment, the Danes denounced all the Swedes and Norwegians as German spies, the Swedes denounced all the Danes and Norwegians, and the Norwegians denounced all the Danes and Swedes. The only Finn was jugged at Kirkwall, and most of the Britons of various factions went ashore there, but the Walrus and his adjutant remained aboard, and during the trip across the

North Sea to what was then Christiania, the first stop on the final lap to Copenhagen, he gave one of his most impressive exhibitions. The principal dish at lunch that day was a so-called suckling pig large enough to have grandchildren: it was garnished with links of sausages, stuffed with bread crumbs and fine herbs, and had in its maw an apple so large that it seemed to have choked to death. The Walrus sawed off both its head and tail, and with the tail got its whole left hind leg, including the ham. This herculean helping he tamped down with a dozen sausages and about two quarts of the stuffing. While he was gobbling away a steward rushed in with the news that a German submarine was in sight, and we all ran on deck to get a look at it, and make our peace with our Maker. Somewhat to our disappointment it merely circled round us twice, and then made off politely. When we got back to the dining-room the Walrus was helping himself to the forequarters of the pig, and excavating another quart of stuffing.

We got to Christiania (now Oslo) the next evening immediately after dinner, and the three waiters at the doctor's table went ashore at once, leaving the Walrus only half way through his mountain of Danish pastry. The rest of us followed soon afterward, eager for a tilt at the night life of Henrik Ibsen's old home-town, but it turned out to be under four feet of snow, and pretty dismal. Worse, something on the order of Prohibition had been clamped down a week or so before, and the only spot we could find that was open and functioning was the main dining-room of the Grand Hotel, a huge chamber with a plush carpet and tarnished gilt lighting fixtures, about as cheering as the slumber-room of a mortician. After we had swallowed some bad beer and looked at the favorite chair of Ibsen we took to plodding about in the snow, hoping against hope that we would hear the sound of revelry somewhere else. We never did, but twice we caught sight of our three waiters and judged enviously that they must have been more lucky. They were crowded into a decrepit taxicab with three girls who had certainly not come from the Y.W.C.A., and as they passed us they gave us loud and boozy greetings, but did not invite us to join them. The next morning, when the ship cast off for Copenhagen and we came down for breakfast, we heard the story of their evening's adventures. This was before the German inflation, but Mexico, always forward-looking, had already gone off the gold standard, and in New York the boys had picked up a couple of hatsful of fifty-peso Mexican greenbacks at a quarter of a cent on the dollar. Two of these greenbacks, we learned, had paid for their whole entertainment in Christiania, though it included wine, women and song. The girls, not knowing about Mexico's forehandedness and assuming that a peso was still worth half a Norwegian crown, had provided all the drinks of the evening, the taxi hire, square meals for six, and the room rent — and even returned $3 change in sound crowns, then still worth 25 cents apiece.

This news got about before the three waiters themselves showed up. When they marched in with their trays, and the Walrus stretched out his mighty hooks to grab them, all the other men at the doctor's table leaped up and gave them three cheers, such being the natural hatred of men for women. And at lunch that day the three Danes and two Swedes at the table opened a couple of magnums of champagne in their honor, such being the natural hatred of all other Scandinavians for Norwegians.

XIII

GORE

IN THE CARIBBEES

[*1917*]

No reporter of my generation, whatever his genius, ever really rated spats and a walking-stick until he had covered both a lynching and a revolution. The first, by the ill-favor of the gods, I always missed, usually by an inch. How often, alas, alas, did I strain and puff my way to some Christian hamlet of the Chesapeake Bay littoral, by buggy, farm-wagon or pack-mule, only to discover that an anti-social sheriff had spirited the blackamoor away, leaving nothing but a seething vacuum behind. Once, as I was on my travels, the same thing happened in the charming town of Springfield, Mo., the Paris and Gomorrah of the Ozarks. I was at dinner at the time with the late Edson K. Bixby, editor of the Springfield *Leader*, along with Paul Patterson and Henry M. Hyde, my colleagues of the Baltimore *Sunpapers*. When the alarm reached us we abandoned our victuals instantly, and leaped and galloped downtown to the jail. By the time we got there, though it was in less than three minutes, the cops had loaded the candidate — he was a white man — into their hurry-wagon and made off for Kansas City, and the lynching mob had been reduced to a hundred or so half-grown youths, a couple of pedlars selling hot-dogs and American flags, and a squawking herd of fascinated but disappointed children.

I had rather better luck with revolutions, though I covered only one, and that one I walked into by a sort of accident. The year was 1917 and I was returning from a whiff of World War I in a Spanish ship that had sailed from La Coruña, Spain, ten days before and was hoping, eventually, to get to Havana. It was, at the moment, somewhat in the maze of the Bahamas, but a wireless reached it nevertheless, and that wireless was directed to me and came from the *Sunpaper* office in Baltimore. It said, in brief, that a revolution had broken out in Cuba, that both sides were doing such rough lying that no one north of the Straits of Florida could make out what it was about, and that a series of succinct and illuminating dispatches describing its issues and personalities would be appreciated. I wirelessed back that the wishes of my superiors were commands, and then sent another wireless to a friend in Havana, Captain Asmus Leonhard, marine superintendent of the Munson Line, saying that I itched to see him the instant my ship made port. Captain Leonhard was a Dane of enormous knowledge but parsimonious speech, and I had a high opinion of his sagacity. He knew everyone worth knowing in Latin America, and thousands who were not, and his estimates of them seldom took more than three words. " A burglar," he would say, characterizing a general played up by all the North American newspapers as the greatest trans-Rio Grande hero since Bolívar, or " a goddam fraud," alluding to a new president of Colombia, San Salvador or Santo Domingo, and that was all. His reply to my wireless was in his usual manner. It said: " Sure."

When the Spanish ship, after groping about for two or three days in Exuma Sound, the North-East Providence Channel, the Tongue of Ocean and various other strangely-named Bahaman waterways, finally made Havana and passed the Morro, a smart young mulatto in Captain Leonhard's launch put out from shore, took me aboard his craft, and whisked me through the customs. The captain himself was waiting in front of the Pasaje Hotel in the Prado, eating a plate of Spanish bean-soup and simultaneously smoking a Romeo y Julietta cigar. " The issues in the revolution," he said, tackling the business in hand at once, " are simple. Menocal, who calls himself a Conservative, is president, and

José Miguel Gomez, who used to be president and calls himself a Liberal, wants to make a come-back. That is the whole story. José Miguel says that when Menocal was reëlected last year the so-called Liberals were chased away from the so-called polls by the so-called army. On the other hand, Menocal says that José Miguel is a porch-climber and ought to be chased out of the island. Both are right."

It seemed clear enough, and I prepared to write a dispatch at once, but Captain Leonhard suggested that perhaps it might be a good idea for me to see Menocal first, and hear the official version in full. We were at the palace in three minutes, and found it swarming with dignitaries. Half of them were army officers in uniform, with swords, and the other half were functionaries of the secretariat. They pranced and roared all over the place, and at intervals of a few seconds more officers would dash up in motor-cars and muscle and whoop their way into the president's office. These last, explained Captain Leonhard, were couriers from the front, for José Miguel, having taken to the bush, was even now surrounded down in Santa Clara province, and there were high hopes that he would be nabbed anon. Despite all the hurly-burly it took only ten minutes for the captain to get me an audience with *el presidente.* I found His Excellency calm and amiable. He spoke English fluently, and was far from reticent. José Miguel, he said, was a fiend in human form who hoped by his treasons to provoke American intervention, and so upset the current freely-chosen and impeccably virtuous government. This foul plot would fail. The gallant Cuban army, which had never lost either a battle or a war, had the traitor cornered, and within a few days he would be chained up among the lizards in the fortress of La Cabaña, waiting for the firing-squad and trying in vain to make his peace with God.

So saying, *el presidente* bowed me out, at the same time offering to put a motor-car and a secretary at my disposal. It seemed a favorable time to write my dispatch, but Captain Leonhard stayed me. "First," he said, "you had better hear what the revolutionists have to say." "The revolutionists!" I exclaimed. "I thought they were out in Santa Clara, surrounded by the army." "Some are," said the captain, "but some ain't. Let us take a hack." So we took a hack and were presently worming our way down the narrow street called Obispo. The captain called a halt in front of a bank, and we got out. "I'll wait here in the bank," he said, "and you go upstairs to Room 309. Ask for Dr. —— " and he whispered a name. "Who is this Dr. ——?" I whispered back. "He is the head of the revolutionary junta," replied the captain. "Mention my name, and he will tell you all about it."

I followed orders, and was soon closeted with the doctor — a very tall, very slim old man with a straggling beard and skin the color of cement.

While we gabbled various persons rushed in and out of his office, most of them carrying papers which they slapped upon his desk. In a corner a young Cuban girl of considerable sightliness banged away at a typewriter. The doctor, like *el presidente,* spoke excellent English, and appeared to be in ebullient spirits. He had trustworthy agents, he gave me to understand, in the palace, some of them in high office. He knew what was going on in the American embassy. He got carbons of all official telegrams from the front. The progress of events there, he said, was extremely favorable to the cause of reform. José Miguel, though somewhat bulky for field service, was a military genius comparable to Joffre or Hindenburg, or even to Hannibal or Alexander, and would soon be making monkeys of the generals of the army. As for Menocal, he was a fiend in human form who hoped to provoke American intervention, and thereby make his corrupt and abominable régime secure.

All this naturally struck me as somewhat unusual, though as a newspaper reporter I was supposed to be incapable of surprise. Here, in the very heart and gizzard of Havana, within sight and hearing of thousands, the revolutionists were maintaining what amounted to open headquarters, and their boss wizard was talking freely, and indeed in a loud voice, to a stranger whose only introduction had been, so to speak, to ask for Joe. I ventured to inquire of the doctor if there were not some danger that his gold-fish globe of a hideaway would be discovered. "Not much," he said. "The army is hunting for us, but the army is so stupid as to be virtually idiotic. The police know where we are, but they believe we are going to win, and want to keep their jobs afterward." From this confidence the doctor proceeded to boasting. "In ten days," he said, "we'll have Menocal jugged in La Cabaña. Shoot him? No; it would be too expensive. The New York banks that run him have plenty of money. If we let him live they will come across."

When I rejoined the captain downstairs I suggested again that it was high time for me to begin composing my dispatch, and this time he agreed. More, he hauled me down to the cable office, only a block or two away, and there left me. "If you get into trouble," he said, "call me up at the Pasaje. I'll be taking my nap, but the clerk will wake me if you need me." I found the cable office very comfortable and even luxurious. There were plenty of desks and typewriters, and when I announced myself I was invited to make myself free of them. Moreover, as I sat down and began to unlimber my prose a large brass spittoon was wheeled up beside me, apparently as a friendly concession to my nationality. At other desks a number of other gentlemen were in labor, and I recognized them at once as colleagues, for a newspaper reporter can always spot another, just as a Freemason can spot a Freemason, or a detective a detective. But I didn't know any of them, and fell to work without speaking to them. When my dispatch was finished I took it to the window, and was informed politely that it would have to be submitted to the censor, who occupied, it appeared, a room in the rear.

The censor turned out to be a young Cuban whose English was quite as good as Menocal's or the doctor's, but unhappily he had rules to follow, and I soon found that they were very onerous. While I palavered with him several of the colleagues came up with copy in their hands, and in two minutes an enormous debate was in progress. He was sworn, I soon gathered, to cut out everything even remotely resembling a fact. No names. No dates. Worse, no conjectures, prognostications, divinations. The colleagues, thus robbed of their habitual provender and full of outrage, put up a dreadful uproar, but the censor stood his ground, and presently I slipped away and called up Captain Leonhard. My respect for his influence was higher than ever now, and it had occurred to me that the revolutionists up the street might have a private cable, and that if they had he would undoubtedly be free of it. But when, in response to his order, I met him in front of the Pasaje, he said nothing about a cable, but heaved me instead into a hack. In ten minutes we were aboard an American ship just about to cast off from a wharf down in the region of the customs-house, and he was introducing me to one of the mates. "Tell him what to do," he said, "and he will do it." I told the mate to file my dispatch the instant his ship docked at Key West, he nodded silently and put the copy into an inside pocket, and that was that. Then the siren sounded and the captain and I returned to the pier.

It all seemed so facile that I became somewhat uneasy. Could the mate be trusted? The captain assured me that he could. But what of the ship? Certainly it did not look fit for wrestling with the notorious swells of the Straits of Florida. Its lines suggested that it had started out in life as an excursion boat on the Hudson, and it was plainly in the last stages of decrepitude. I knew that the run to Key West was rather more than a hundred miles, and my guess, imparted to the captain, was that no such craft could make it in less than forty-eight hours. But the captain only laughed. "That old hulk," he said, "is the fastest ship in the Caribbean. If it doesn't hit a log or break in two it will make Key West in five and a half hours." He was right as usual, for that night, just as I was turning in at the Pasaje I received a cable from the *Sunpaper* saying that my treatise on the revolution had begun to run, and was very illuminating and high-toned stuff.

Thereafter, I unloaded all my dissertations in the same manner. Every afternoon I would divert attention by waiting on the censor and filing a dispatch so full of contraband that I knew he would never send it, and then I would go down to the wharf and look up the mate. On the fourth day he was *non est* and I was in a panic, for the captain had gone on a business trip into Pinar del Rio and no one else could help me. But just as the lines were being cast off I caught sight of a likely-looking Americano standing at the gangway and decided to throw myself upon his Christian charity. He responded readily, and my dispatch went through as usual. Thereafter, though the mate never showed up again — I heard later that he was sick in Key West — I always managed to find an accommodating passenger. Meanwhile, the censor's copy-hook accumulated a fine crop of my rejected cablegrams, and mixed with them were scores by the colleagues. Every time I went to the cable office I found the whole corps raising hell, and threatening all sorts of reprisals and revenges. But they seldom got anything through save the official communiqués that issued from the palace at hourly intervals.

These communiqués were prepared by a large staff of press-agents, and were not only couched in extremely florid words but ran to great lengths. I had just come from Berlin, where all that the German General Staff had to say every day, though war was raging on two fronts, was commonly put into no more than 300 words, so this Latin exuberance rather astonished me. But the stuff made gaudy reading, and I sent a lot of it to the *Sunpaper* by mail, for the entertainment and instruction of the gentlemen of the copy-desk. The Cuban mails, of course, were censored like the cable, but the same Americano who carried my afternoon dispatch to Key West was always willing to mail a few long envelopes at the same place. Meanwhile, I hung about the palace, and picked up enough off-record gossip to give my dispatches a pleasant air of verisimilitude, soothing to editors if not to readers. Also, I made daily visits to the headquarters of the revolutionists, and there got a lot of information, some of it sound, to the same end. In three days, such is the quick grasp of the reportorial mind, I knew all the ins and outs of the revolution, and in a week I was fit to write a history of Cuban politics from the days of Diego Velazquez. I was, of course, younger then than I am now, and reporters today are not what they used to be, but into that we need not go.

After a week it began to be plain, even on the evidence supplied by the revolutionists, that the uprising was making heavy weather of it, and when, a day or two later, the palace press-agents announced, in a communiqué running to 8,000 words, that José Miguel Gomez was about to be taken, I joined the colleagues in believing it. We all demanded, of course, to be let in on the final scene, and after a long series of conferences, with speeches by Menocal, half a dozen high army officers, all the press-agents and most of the correspondents, it was so ordered. According to both the palace and the revolutionists, the front was down at Placetas in Santa Clara, 180 miles away, but even in those days there were plenty of Fords in Havana, and it was arranged that a fleet of them should start out the next morning, loaded with correspondents, typewriters and bottled beer. Unhappily, the trip was never made, for at the precise moment the order for it was being issued a dashing colonel in Santa Clara was leading his men in a grand assault upon José Miguel, and after ten minutes of terrific fire and deafening yells the Cuban Hindenburg hoisted his shirt upon the tip of his sword and surrendered. He did not have to take his shirt off for the purpose: it was already hanging upon a guava bush, for he had been preparing for a siesta in his hammock. Why he did not know of the projected attack I could never find out, for he was held incommunicado in La Cabaña until I left Cuba, and neither the palace nor the revolutionists seemed willing to discuss the subject.

The palace press-agents, you may be sure, spit on their hands when they heard the news, and turned out a series of communiqués perhaps unsurpassed in the history of war. Their hot, lascivious rhetoric was still flowing three or four days later, long after poor José Miguel was safely jugged among the lizards and scorpions. I recall one canto of five or six thousand words that included a minute autopsy on the strategy and tactics of the final battle, written by a gifted military pathologist on the staff of the victorious colonel. He described every move in the stealthy approach to José Miguel in the minutest detail, and pitched his analysis in highly graphic and even blood-curdling terms. More than once, it appeared, the whole operation was in dire peril, and a false step might have wrecked it, and thereby delivered Cuba to the wolves. Indeed, it might have been baffled at its very apex and apogee if only José Miguel had had his shirt on. As it was, he could not, according to Latin notions of decorum, lead his men, and in consequence they skedaddled, and he himself was forced to yield his sword to the agents of the New York banks.

The night of the victory was a great night in Havana, and especially at the palace. President Menocal kept open house in the most literal sense: his office door was wide open and anyone was free to rush in and hug him. Thousands did so, including scores of officers arriving home from the front. Some of these officers were indubitably Caucasians, but a great many were of darker shades, including saddle-brown and coffin-black. As they leaped out of their Fords in front of the palace the bystanders fell upon them with patriotic gloats and gurgles, and kissed them on both cheeks. Then they struggled up the grand staircase to *el presidente's* reception-room, and were kissed again by the superior public there assembled. Finally, they leaped into the inner office, and fell to kissing His Excellency and to being kissed by him. It was an exhilarating show, but full of strangeness to a Nordic. I observed two things especially. The first was that, for all the uproar, no one was drunk. The other was that the cops beat up no one.

José Miguel was brought to Havana the next morning, chained up in a hearse, and the palace press-agents announced in a series of ten or fifteen communiqués that he would be tried during the afternoon, and shot at sunrise the day following. The colleagues, robbed of their chance to see his capture, now applied for permission to see him put to death, and somewhat to their surprise it was granted readily. He was to be turned off, it appeared, at 6 a.m. promptly, so they were asked to be at the gate of La Cabaña an hour earlier. Most of them were on hand, but the sentry on watch refused to let them in, and after half an hour's wrangle a young officer came out and said that the execution had been postponed until the next day. But the next day it was put off again, and again the next, and after three or four days no more colleagues showed up at the gate. It was then announced by the palace literati that President Menocal had commuted the sentence to solitary confinement for life in a dungeon on the Cayos de la Doce Leguas off the south coast, where the mosquitoes were as large as bullfrogs, along with confiscation of all the culprit's property, whether real, personal or mixed, and the perpetual loss of his civil rights, such as they were.

But even this turned out to be only tall talk, for President Menocal was a very humane man, and pretty soon he reduced José Miguel's sentence to fifty years, and then to fifteen, and then to six, and then to two. Soon after that he wiped out the jugging altogether, and substituted a fine — first of $1,000,000, then of $250,000, and then of $50,000. The common belief was that José Miguel was enormously rich, but this was found to be an exaggeration. When I left Cuba he was still protesting that the last and lowest fine was far beyond his means, and in the end, I believe, he was let off with the confiscation of his yacht, a small craft then laid up with engine trouble. When he died in 1921 he had resumed his old place among the acknowledged heroes of his country. Twenty years later Menocal joined him in Valhalla.

XIV

ROMANTIC

INTERMEZZO

[*1920*]

TAKE wine, women and song, add plenty of A-No. 1 victuals, the belch and bellow of oratory, a balmy but stimulating climate and a whiff of patriotism, and it must be obvious that you have a dose with a very powerful kick in it. This, precisely, was the dose that made the Democratic national convention of 1920, holden in San Francisco, the most charming in American annals. No one who was present at its sessions will ever forget it. It made history for its voluptuous loveliness, just as the Baltimore convention of 1912 made history for its infernal heat, and the New York convention of 1924 for its 103 ballots and its unparalleled din. Whenever I meet an old-timer who took part in it we fall into maudlin reminiscences of it, and tears drop off the ends of our noses. It came within an inch of being perfect. It was San Francisco's brave answer to the Nazi-inspired earthquake of April 18, 1906.

The whole population shared in the credit for it, and even the powers and principalities of the air had a hand, for they provided the magnificent weather, but chief praise went justly to the Hon. James Rolph, Jr., then and for eleven years afterward mayor of the town. In 1920, indeed, he had already been mayor for nine years, and in 1931, after five terms of four years each in that office, he was promoted to the dignity of Governor of California. He was a man of bold imagination and spacious ideas. More than anyone else he was responsible for the superb hall in which the convention was held, and more than any other he deserved thanks for the humane and enlightened entertainment of the delegates and alternates. The heart of that entertainment was a carload of Bourbon whiskey, old, mellow and full of pungent but delicate tangs — in brief, the best that money could buy.

The persons who go to Democratic national conventions seldom see such wet goods; in truth, they had never seen any before, and they have never seen any since. The general rule is to feed them the worst obtainable, and at the highest prices they can be cajoled and swindled into paying. Inasmuch as large numbers of them are Southerners, and most of the rest have Southern sympathies, it is assumed that they will drink anything, however revolting, provided only it have enough kick. In preparation for their quadrennial gathering to nominate a candidate for the Presidency the wholesale booze-sellers of the country ship in the dregs of their cellars — rye whiskey in which rats have drowned, Bourbon contaminated with arsenic and ptomaines, corn fresh from the still, gin that is three-fourths turpentine, and rum rejected as too corrosive by the West Indian embalmers. This stuff the Democrats put away with loud hosannas — but only for a few days. After that their livers give out, they lose their tempers, and the country is entertained with a rough-house in the grand manner. There has been such a rough-house at every Democratic national convention since Jackson's day, save only the *Ja*-convention at Chicago in 1940 and the incomparable gathering at San Francisco in 1920. The scene at the latter was one of universal peace and lovey-dovey, and every Democrat went home on his own legs, with his soul exultant and both his ears intact and functioning.

The beauty of this miracle was greatly enhanced by the fact that it was unexpected. Prohibition had gone into force only five months before the convention was scheduled to meet, and the Democrats arrived in San Francisco full of miserable forebodings. Judging by what they had already experienced at home, they assumed that the convention booze would be even worse than usual; indeed, most of them were so uneasy about it that they brought along supplies of their own. During the five months they had got used to hair oil, Jamaica ginger and sweet spirits of nitre, but they feared that the San Francisco booticians, abandoning all reason, would proceed to paint remover and sheep dip. What a surprise awaited them! What a deliverance was at hand! The moment they got to their hotels they were waited upon by small committees of refined and well-dressed ladies, and asked to state their desires. The majority, at the start, were so suspicious that they kicked the ladies out; they feared entrapment by what were then still called revenuers. But the bolder fellows took a chance — and a few hours later the glad word was everywhere. No matter what a delegate ordered he got Bourbon — but it was Bourbon of the very first chop, Bourbon aged in contented barrels of the finest white oak, Bourbon of really ultra and super quality. It came in quart bottles on the very heels of the committee of ladies — and there was no bill attached. It was offered to the visitors with the compliments of Mayor James Rolph, Jr.

The effects of that Bourbon were so wondrous that it is easy to exaggerate them in retrospect. There were, of course, other links in the chain of causation behind the phenomena I am about to describe. One, as I have hinted, was the weather — a series of days so sunshiny and caressing, so cool and exhilarating that living through them was like rolling on meads of asphodel. Another was the hall in which the convention was held — a new city auditorium so spacious, so clean, so luxurious in its comforts and so beautiful in its decorations that the assembled politicoes felt like sailors turned loose in the most gorgeous bordellos of Paris. I had just come from the Republican national convention in Chicago, and was thus keen to the contrast. The hall in Chicago was an old armory that had been used but lately for prize fights, dog shows and a third-rate circus, and it still smelled of pugs, kennels and elephants. Its walls and gallery railings were covered to the last inch with shabby flags and bunting that seemed to have come straight from a bankrupt street carnival. Down in the catacombs beneath it the victualling accommodations were of a grab-it-and-run, eat-it-if-you-can character, and the rooms marked " Gents " followed the primordial design of Sir John Harington as given in his " Metamorphosis of Ajax," published in 1596. To police this foul pen there was a mob of ward heelers from the Chicago slums, wearing huge badges, armed with clubs, and bent on packing both the gallery and the floor with their simian friends.

The contrast presented by the San Francisco hall was so vast as to be astounding. It was as clean as an operating room, or even a brewery, and its decorations were all of a chaste and restful character. The walls were hung, not with garish bunting, but with fabrics in low tones of gray and green, and in the whole place only one flag was visible. Downstairs, in the spacious basement, there were lunch-counters served by lovely young creatures in white uniforms, and offering the whole repertory of West Coast delicacies at cut-rate prices. The Johns were lined with mirrors, and each was staffed with shoe-shiners, suit-pressers and hat-cleaners, and outfitted with automatic weighing-machines, cigar-lighters, devices releasing a squirt of Jockey Club perfume for a cent, and recent files of all the principal newspapers of the United States. The police arrangements almost deserved the epithet of dainty. There were no ward heelers armed with clubs, and even the uniformed city police were confined to a few garrison posts, concealed behind marble pillars. All ordinary ushering and trouble-shooting was done by a force of cuties dressed like the waitresses in the basement, and each and every one of them was well worth a straining of the neck. They were armed with little white wands, and every wand was tied with a blue ribbon, signifying law and order. When one of these babies glided into a jam of delegates with her wand upraised they melted as if she had been a man-eating tiger, but with this difference: that instead of making off with screams of terror they yielded as if to soft music, their eyes rolling ecstatically and their hearts going pitter-pat.

But under it all, of course, lay the soothing pharmacological effect of Jim Rolph's incomparable

Bourbon. Delegates who, at all previous Democratic conventions, had come down with stone in the liver on the second day were here in the full tide of health and optimism on the fifth. There was not a single case of mania à potu from end to end of the gathering, though the place swarmed with men who were subject to it. Not a delegate took home gastritis. The Bourbon was so pure that it not only did not etch and burn them out like the horrible hooches they were used to; it had a positively therapeutic effect, and cured them of whatever they were suffering from when they got to town. Day by day they swam in delight. The sessions of the convention, rid for once of the usual quarreling and caterwauling, went on like a conference of ambassadors, and in the evenings the delegates gave themselves over to amicable conversation and the orderly drinking of healths. The climax came on June 30, the day set apart for putting candidates for the Presidency in nomination. It was, in its way, the loveliest day of the whole fortnight, with a cloudless sky, the softest whisper of a breeze from the Pacific, and a sun that warmed without heating. As the delegates sat in their places listening to the speeches and the music they could look out of the open doors of the hall to the Golden Gate, and there see a fleet of warships that had been sent in by the Hon. Josephus Daniels, then Secretary of the Navy, to entertain them with salutes and manoeuvres.

There was an excellent band in the hall, and its leader had been instructed to dress in every speaker with appropriate music. If a gentleman from Kentucky arose, then the band played " My Old Kentucky Home "; if he was followed by one from Indiana, then it played " On the Banks of the Wabash." Only once during the memorable day did the leader make a slip, and that was when he greeted a Georgia delegate with " Marching Through Georgia," but even then he quickly recovered himself and slid into " At a Georgia Campmeeting." An entirely new problem confronted him as the morning wore on, for it was at San Francisco in 1920 that the first lady delegates appeared at a Democratic national convention. His test came when the earliest bird among these stateswomen got the chairman's eye. What she arose to say I do not recall, but I remember that she was a Mrs. FitzGerald of Massachusetts, a very handsome woman. As she appeared on the platform, the leader let go with " Oh, You Beautiful Doll! " The delegates and alternates, struck by the artful patness of the selection, leaped to their legs and cheered, and La FitzGerald's remarks, whatever they were, were received with almost delirious enthusiasm. The next female up was Mrs. Izetta Jewel Brown of West Virginia, a former actress who knew precisely how to walk across a stage and what clothes were for. When the delegates and alternates saw her they were stricken dumb with admiration, but when the band leader gave her "Oh, What a Pal Was Mary," they cut loose with yells that must have been heard half way to San José.

It was not these ladies, however, who made top score on that memorable day, but the Hon. Al Smith of New York. Al, in those days, was by no means the national celebrity that he was to become later. He had already, to be sure, served a year of his first term as Governor of New York, but not many people west of Erie, Pa., had ever heard of him, and to most of the delegates at San Francisco he was no more than a vague name. Thus there was little sign of interest when the Hon. W. Bourke Cockran arose to put him in nomination — the first of his three attempts upon the White House. Cockran made a good speech, but it fell flat, nor did the band leader help things when he played "Tammany" at its close, for Tammany Hall suggested only Romish villainies to the delegates from the Bible country. But when, as if seeing his error, the leader quickly swung into "The Sidewalks of New York" a murmur of appreciation ran through the hall, and by the time the band got to the second stanza someone in a gallery began to sing. The effect of that singing, as the old-time reporters used to say, was electrical. In ten seconds a hundred other voices had joined in, and in a minute the whole audience was bellowing the familiar words. The band played six or eight stanzas, and then switched to "Little Annie Rooney," and then to

" The Bowery," and then to " A Bicycle Built For Two," and then to " Maggie Murphy's Home," and so on down the long line of ancient waltz-songs. Here the leader showed brilliantly his subtle mastery of his art. Not once did he change to four-four time: it would have broken the spell. But three-four time, the sempiternal measure of amour, caught them all where they were tenderest, and for a solid hour the delegates and alternates sang and danced.

The scene was unprecedented in national conventions and has never been repeated since, though many another band leader has tried to put it on: what he lacked was always the aid of Jim Rolph's Bourbon. The first delegate who grabbed a lady politico and began to prance up the aisle was full of it, and so, for all I know, was the lady politico. They were joined quickly by others, and in ten minutes Al was forgotten, the convention was in recess, and a ball was in progress. Not many of the delegates, of course, were equal to actual waltzing, but in next to no time a ground rule was evolved which admitted any kind of cavorting that would fit into the music, so the shindig gradually gathered force and momentum, and by the end of the first half hour the only persons on the floor who were not dancing were a few antisocial Hardshell Baptists from Mississippi, and a one-legged war veteran from Ohio. For a while the chairman, old Joe Robinson, made formal attempts to restore order, but after that he let it run, and run it did until the last hoofer was exhausted. Then a young man named Franklin D. Roosevelt got up to second Al's nomination. He made a long and earnest speech on the heroic achievements of the Navy in the late war, and killed Al's boom then and there.

That great and singular day was a Wednesday, and the bosses of the convention made plans the next morning to bring its proceedings to a close on Saturday. But the delegates and alternates simply refused to agree. The romantic tunes of "East Side, West Side" and "A Bicycle Built For Two" were still sounding in their ears, and their veins still bulged and glowed with Jim Rolph's Bourbon. The supply of it seemed to be unlimited. Day by day, almost hour by hour, the ladies' committee produced more. Thus Thursday passed in happy abandon, and then Friday. On Saturday someone proposed boldly that the convention adjourn over the week-end, and the motion was carried by a vote of 998 to 26. That afternoon the delegates and alternates, each packing a liberal supply of the Bourbon, entered into taxicabs and set out to see what was over the horizon. San Francisco was perfect, but they sweated for new worlds, new marvels, new adventures. On the Monday following some of them were roped by the police in places more than a hundred miles away, and started back to their duties in charge of trained nurses. One taxicab actually reached Carson City, Nev., and another was reported, probably apocryphally, in San Diego. I myself, though I am an abstemious man, awoke on Sunday morning on the beach at Half Moon Bay, which is as far from San Francisco as Peekskill is from New York. But that was caused, not by Jim Rolph's Bourbon, but by George Sterling's grappo, a kind of brandy distilled from California grape skins, with the addition of strychnine.

After the delegates went home at last the Methodists of San Francisco got wind of the Bourbon and started a noisy public inquiry into its provenance. Jim Rolph, who was a very dignified man, let them roar on without deigning to notice them, even when they alleged that it had been charged to the town smallpox hospital, and offered to prove that there had not been a case of smallpox there since 1897. In due time he came up for reëlection, and they renewed their lying and unChristian attack. As a result he was reëlected almost unanimously, and remained in office, as I have noted, until 1931. In that year, as I have also noted, he was promoted by the appreciative people of all California to the highest place within their gift, and there he remained, to the satisfaction of the whole human race, until his lamented death in 1934.

XV

OLD HOME DAY

[*1922*]

IN the Autumn of 1922, being at large in Europe, I was assigned by the Baltimore *Sunpaper* to go to the island of Wieringen in the Zuider Zee to have a look at the German Crown Prince, then interned there. I recall that I had a pleasant day with him, but what he had to say I forget. Indeed, my only clear memory of the trip has to do with its difficulties, not with its object. On the map Wieringen looks to be almost as conveniently located as Staten Island, and its airline distance from Amsterdam can't be more than forty miles, but it took me two whole days and nights to get there and back, and I had to use every common means of conveyance save wheelbarrows and camels. Most of all, I remember that one of the two nights *en route* was spent in a little town called Den Helder, at the northernmost tip of the Holland mainland — the most depressing place, not excepting Waycross, Ga., and Elwood, Ind., that I have ever encountered.

Den Helder lies just under the dike that keeps the North Sea off the flat farmlands behind it, and serves in Summer as a bathing place for the inferior bourgeoisie of the North Holland towns. How these customers manage to bathe there I do not know and can't figure out, for the seaward side of the dike slopes down at an angle of at least 40 degrees and is paved with jagged and enormous cobblestones, brought in from Norway to turn the teeth of the sea. But that is neither here nor there, for when I saw the place it was well along in September, and all the Summer visitors had gone home. There was only one hotel open, and in it I was given a room on the top floor, just high enough in the air for me to see over the crest of the dike. As I glanced out of my window to get my bearings a wave was coming in from the northwest, which is to say, from the very bowels of the North Sea. It looked, to my unpractised eye, to be at least 200 feet high, and when it struck the dike and was busted and baffled by the cobblestones it made a roar like a whole herd of Niagaras. The hotel trembled so violently that I was knocked off my feet, and the ensuing reverberations must have shaken the villages as far south as Alkmaar.

Obviously, it would be impossible to sleep in that room without the use of drugs, and inasmuch as I had no opium or chloroform on me I returned downstairs to the coffee-room to find out what offered there. To my astonishment I found that none of the waiters on duty could speak English, nor, indeed, any other language that I was acquainted with, even by hearsay. I tried them with bad German, worse French, downright pathological Spanish, and even snatches of Danish, Russian, Czech, Turkish and Swahili, but they kept on spreading their hands and shaking their heads. Finally, I opened my mouth, pointed into it, made a show of swallowing, and indicated my stomach, whereupon they rushed off in a body — and returned anon with a cup of coffee! I must have lost consciousness momentarily, for by the time I found myself jawing them again there was a new man among them and he was addressing me in German so atrocious that I understood it perfectly. He was, he said, a waiter also, but he had been on duty since 6 a.m. and was preparing to go to bed when his colleagues called him. I thanked him for his kindness, asked him to bring me three large glasses of the best beer in the house, and when he returned with them invited him to sit down and drink one of them with me. He accepted politely, and turned out to be a very entertaining and even instructive fellow. We sat there together, in fact, for four hours, and during the first of them he gave me an account of his life in considerable detail. I forget most of it, but I recall that he said he was a native of a village that was half in Holland and half in Germany, and that he had had to clear out of it because of a difficulty with the German *Polizei.* At that very moment, he went on, there was a reward of fifty marks outstanding against him, dead or alive. He said he had come to Den Helder because it was the most remote spot in the settled parts of Europe, and a rival, almost, to Spitsbergen and Archangel. No stranger had been seen in it between the Napoleonic wars and the arrival of the Crown Prince at Wieringen.

From such matters he went on to consider larger affairs, and was presently discoursing upon a theme that has always interested me — the differences between races. There was a good deal of public talk at the time about Leagues of Nations, international peace treaties, and such like hallucinations, and on them he brought to bear a blistering scorn and what seemed to me to be excellent sense. They would always and inevitably run aground, he said, on the rocks of inter-racial enmity — a thing as natural to mankind, and almost as hard to get rid of, as thirst or lying. The Germans and the Dutch, he said, though they had to live side by side, hated each other with a hatred that was fathomless and implacable, and he himself, as a sort of neutral or mongrel, hated both. This enmity, he continued, had little basis in logic. It was simply a matter of taste, and its springs lay in trifles — tones of voice, ways of trimming the hair, the cut of clothes, table manners, and so on. Nor did it rage only between definitely different races;

it also split every race into an endless series of hostile factions. " Holland," he said, " is a small country, but the people of one part dislike those of another almost as violently as a Bavarian dislikes a Prussian. And when a Hollander goes abroad — say to the Dutch East Indies or to America — and then comes home for a visit, he finds that he dislikes them all." In witness whereof he told me a curious story, substantially as follows.

There was living down in the *Polder* near Den Helder — the *Polder* is the flat farmland, criss-crossed with tiny canals, that lies below the dikes — an old farm-wife whose only son had long ago emigrated to America, and there done very well by himself in the Dutch colony of Michigan. He never forgot his old mother, but sent her money constantly, and she lived very well on the ancestral farm — a place of eight or ten acres —, with the daughter of a neighbor to wait on her. Her house, indeed, was a kind of show-place, for it was furnished with all the swellest goods of the Amsterdam department-stores. She had a parlor so jammed with marble-topped and mahoganized furniture that it was impossible to get into it, and in her garret were scores of feather-beds — still the touchstones of wealth in all parts of rural Europe north of the Alps. When she gave a coffee-party to her buddies among the other farm wives of the neighborhood, there was so much on the table that fifty per cent. of the guests were laid up the next day.

She was Heaven's gift to the pastor of the village church. Whenever he developed a brisk appetite, which was often, she would set him a banquet that bulged him like a pouter-pigeon, and she kept him supplied with American Bull Durham for his pipe, sent to her by her loving and dutiful son.

This son, however, had not been home for years. For one thing, he had been busy building up a lime and cement business in a town near Grand Rapids, for another thing he had gone into politics, and for a third thing he had got married. His bride was a girl of Dutch ancestry, but born in Kalamazoo — a high-school graduate of aesthetic leanings, with some talent for interior decoration and the violoncello. Their affectionate coöperation had blessed them with a daughter, and the child was now four years old. The war having prospered both politics and the lime and cement business in Michigan, the son decided, in 1921, to make a long-overdue visit to his aged mother, and to take his wife and daughter along. They arrived at Rotterdam in November of that year, and early the next morning proceeded northward by train. It was a fast train, as such things go in Holland — in fact, it was known as the Kanonskogel, or Cannonball — but it took all day to make the trip from Rotterdam to the nose of North Holland, and by the time the pilgrims got to the farm it was pitch dark.

The old lady, of course, was ready with a big welcome, and had put on her best Sunday clothes for the purpose. Moreover, she and her slavey had prepared a stupendous meal to refresh the visitors after their long journey. Yet more, she had asked her friend, the pastor, to grace and bedizen the occasion, and he was present in his full ecclesiastical habiliments, with his beard beautifully currycombed. As the visitors were set down at the door the old lady rushed out, grabbed her precious grandchild, and gave it a tremendous hug. Unhappily, the child was worn out by the long train-trip, and became alarmed by its grandma's strange costume, so it set up a shrill squawk, and by the time the party got into the house it was howling in a wild and deafening manner. Its father and mother combined to quiet it, first trying soothing and then clouting its bottom, but it took them ten minutes to shut off its caterwauling, and meanwhile the victuals had to wait.

When the party finally got to the table the pastor arose and let go with a prayer that was of truly appalling range and length. He not only prayed earnestly for all the persons present; he also prayed for the Dutch royal family, for Woodrow Wilson, for Clemenceau, for Lloyd-George, for the Dutch colonists in Michigan, for the lime and cement business, and for the heathen everywhere. And then, having got over all that ground, he prayed *against* the ex-Kaiser, the Crown Prince at Wieringen, Hindenburg, Ludendorff and all the other German generals, with occasional flings at the Austrians, the Bulgarians and the Turks. The bride from Kalamazoo, knowing little Dutch, could barely get the drift of it, so she devoted herself to a sly examination of the room they sat in. Unfortunately, there was only a single oil-lamp on the table, and in consequence the ceiling, upper walls and far corners were in shadow, but on the wall opposite she could see no less than five lithographs of Queen Wilhelmina — apparently a series showing her gradual increase in bulk from 175 pounds to 250.

The table itself was sufficiently lighted for a more minute survey. She counted six hams, a huge pile of black, red, gray and green sausages, a bowl containing at least 200 boiled eggs, a fish so large that it looked to be a dolphin, a loaf of rye bread two feet long and a foot thick, and no less than ten cheeses, some of them of the size of suitcases. She had been hungry when she arrived, but now her appetite oozed out of her. Her husband ate diligently, urged on by his loving old mother, but after he had sampled five of the cheeses he began to look faint, and begged for air. As for the child, it remained quiet enough until the old lady, having stoked the pastor, sawed off a slab of rye bread two inches thick, added a huge stratum of ham, and bade it eat. Its response was to resume its caterwauling, with the addition of loud demands for a plate of shredded wheat and prunes, its usual supper in Michigan.

The conversation at table, of course, was somewhat labored. The son tried to translate his mother's remarks, and the much longer observations of the pastor, but his wife's mind kept straying from the subjects they treated, and the child went on whining and whimpering. After the meal was got down at last and the pastor had prayed again — this time at less length, for he was pretty well gorged — the old lady suggested sensibly that the little girl must be tired out, and had better be put to bed. Its mother agreed joyfully, and a march to the upper regions of the farmhouse began. It led up a stairway as dark as the family entrance to an old-time Raines law hotel. The grandmother went ahead with a lamp fetched from the kitchen, but its light was hidden by her body, and the child began yowling again in a frantic manner, the while her mother tried to quiet her, and her father, who brought up the rear, began swearing dismally in English and Dutch. The yowling continued while the undressing was going on, but the grand climax of the evening did not come until it was finished. Once the little girl was in her nightie her poor grandmother claimed the privilege of laying her in the bed awaiting her — the most sumptuous between Haarlem and the island of Texel. It was stuffed with at least a hundred pounds of the finest goose feathers known to science — not the common ones that go into ordinary feather-beds, but fine pin-feathers from the most delicate and sanitary areas of adolescent geese specially bred and fed for the service. The old lady lifted the child fondly, and then let it drop ever so gently. It gave a single blood-curdling yell — and straightway disappeared!

The waiter told me that such phenomena were not uncommon in the feather-bed country. A really good bed, made of the super-colossal feathers I have described, was as soft as a powder-puff. Getting into it required a complicated technic, and getting out was even more difficult. Why the old lady did not remember this he did not say and I do not know: no doubt she was somewhat addled by the sad failure of her party and the general uproar. Whatever the fact, the child vanished like a stone thrown into water, and at once both its father and its mother leaped in after it, seeking to bring it to the surface and drag it ashore. When it came up at last its little face was purple, its psyche was aflame with complexes, and it was in the full tide of hysterics. So, indeed, was its mother. Grasping her rescued offspring to her breast, she shooed the heart-broken grandmother downstairs, and then sat down to calm it. She remained at that labor, according to the waiter, until nearly 6 a.m. The dawn was reddening when the child finally fell asleep, and the mother fixed it a pallet on the floor. When she got to her own bedroom, and found only the nose of her husband showing, she broke into whoops of her own, and it took him another half hour to get her to bed herself. Even so, she refused to undress, but went into the feathers with all her clothes on, including her shoes.

The waiter said that the rest of the story was brief but melancholy. The poor old grandmother spent a miserable night herself, wondering why her welcome to her son and his family had been such a flop, and trying to puzzle out the strange ways of American-born children. She determined to make amends by setting a breakfast in the most lavish North Holland style — the sort of thing that had brought her son down with grateful bellyaches when he was a boy. To that end she got her slavey out before dawn, and the two of them fell upon the job of preparing it. When her guests came down at last the table was spread even more royally than the evening before. On it stood a jar of every kind of preserves or pickle in her storeroom, and in the center of them was a huge platter covered with forty or fifty fried eggs, sizzling. At one end was a ham to end all hams — it apparently came from a hippopotamus — with a *Blutwurst* and a *Leberwurst* to flank it, and at the other end was a cheese as big as *two* suitcases. The daughter-in-law took one look, and then rushed out into the yard: something analogous to *mal de mer* had fetched her. The child, seeing her flee, ran after her, shrieking piteously, and the son made after the child.

At 9 a.m., continued the waiter, the three boarded the south-bound Cannonball at the nearest flag-stop, with the child still carrying on in a frenzied manner, and ten or twelve hours later they were in Rotterdam. The next day they started back for America — in the same ship that had brought them in only three days before. "The poor old woman," he concluded, "never got over it. She had been blowing about her rich son and his family for months, and now they had walked out on her. Who's fault was it? Nobody's. The pastor laid the whole thing to God, and I believe he was right."

XVI

THE NOBLE EXPERIMENT

[*1924*]

PROHIBITION went into effect on January 16, 1920, and blew up at last on December 5, 1933 — an elapsed time of twelve years, ten months and nineteen days. It seemed almost a geological epoch while it was going on, and the human suffering that it entailed must have been a fair match for that of the Black Death or the Thirty Years' War, but I should say at once that my own share of the blood, sweat and tears was extremely meagre. I was, so far as I have been able to discover, the first man south of the Mason and Dixon line to brew a drinkable home-brew, and as a result my native Baltimore smelled powerfully of malt and hops during the whole horror, for I did not keep my art to myself, but imparted it to anyone who could be trusted

— which meant anyone save a few abandoned Methodists, Baptists and Presbyterians, most of them already far gone in glycosuria, cholelithiasis or gastrohydrorrhea, and all of them soon so low in mind and body that they could be ignored.

My seminary was run on a sort of chain-letter plan. That is to say, I took ten pupils, and then each of the ten took ten, and so on *ad infinitum.* There were dull dogs in Baltimore who went through the course forty or fifty times, under as many different holders of my degrees, and even then never got beyond a nauseous *Malzsuppe,* fit only for policemen and Sunday-school superintendents. But there were others of a much more shining talent, and I put in a great deal of my time in 1921 and 1922 visiting their laboratories, to pass judgment on their brews. They received me with all the deference due to a master, and I was greatly bucked up by their attentions. In fact, those attentions probably saved me from melancholia, for during the whole of the twelve years, ten months and nineteen days I was a magazine editor, and a magazine editor is a man who lives on a sort of spiritual Bataan, with bombs of odium taking him incessantly from the front and torpedoes of obloquy harrying him astern.

But I would not have you think that I was anything like dependent, in that abominable time, upon home-brew, or that I got down any really formidable amount of it. To be sure, I had to apply my critical powers to many thousands of specimens, but I always took them in small doses, and was careful to blow away a good deal of the substance with the foam. This home-brew, when drinkable at all, was a striking proof of the indomitable spirit of man, but in the average case it was not much more. Whenever the mood to drink purely voluptuously was on me I preferred, of course, the product of professional brewmasters, and, having been born lucky, I usually found it. Its provenance, in those days, was kept a kind of military secret, but now that the nightmare is over and jails no longer yawn I do not hesitate to say that, in so far as my own supply went, most of it came from the two lowermost tiers of Pennsylvania counties. Dotted over that smiling pastoral landscape there were groups of small breweries that managed successfully, by means that we need not go into, to stall off the Prohibition agents, and I had the privilege and honor of getting down many a carboy of their excellent product both in Baltimore, where I lived, and in New York, where I had my office.

When I say New York I mean the city in its largest sense — the whole metropolitan region. As a matter of fact, the malt liquor on tap on the actual island of Manhattan was usually bad, and often downright poisonous. When I yearned for a quaff of the real stuff I went to Union Hill, N. J., and if not to Union Hill, then to Hoboken. Both of these great outposts radiated a bouquet of malt and hops almost as pungent as Baltimore's, and in Union Hill there was a beer-house that sticks in my memory as the most comfortable I have ever encountered on this earth. Its beers were perfect, its victuals were cheap and nourishing, its chairs were designed by osteological engineers specializing in the structure of the human pelvis, and its waiters, Axel, Otto, Julius and Raymond, were experts at their science.[1] This incomparable dump was discovered by the late Philip Goodman, then transiently a theatrical manager on Broadway and all his life a fervent beer-drinker, and he and I visited it every time I was in New York, which was pretty often. We would ease into our canons' stalls in the early evening and continue in residence until Axel, Otto, Julius and Raymond began to snore in their corner and the colored maintenance engineer, Willie, turned his fire-hose into the washroom. Then back by taxi to Weehawken, from Weehawken to Forty-second street by the six-minute ferry, and from Forty-second street by taxi again to the quick, lordly sleep of quiet minds and pure hearts.

The fact that the brews on tap in that Elysium came from lower Pennsylvania naturally suggested an expedition to the place of their origin, and

1 Raymond, like Axel, was from upper Schleswig-Holstein, and hence technically a Dane. I naturally assumed that his baptismal name was an Americanized form of the old Teutonic name of Reimund, signifying a sagacious councilor. But one night he told me that his father, a *Stadtpfeiffer,* had named him after the " Raymond " overture by Ambrose Thomas, a work he greatly admired.

Goodman and I laid many plans for making the trip in his car. But every time we started out we dropped in on Axel, Otto, Julius and Raymond for stirrup cups, and that was as far as we ever got. Alone, however, I once visited Harrisburg on newspaper business, and there had the felicity of drinking close to the *Urquell*. That was in the primitive days when New York still bristled with peepholes and it was impossible to get into a strange place without a letter from a judge, but in Harrisburg there were no formalities. I simply approached a traffic cop and asked him where reliable stuff was to be had. " Do you see that kaif there? " he replied, pointing to the corner. " Well, just go in and lay down your money. If you don't like it, come back and I'll give you another one." I liked it well enough, and so did not trouble him further.

I should add, however, that I once came so near going dry in Pennsylvania, and in the very midst of a huge fleet of illicit breweries, that the memory of it still makes me shiver. This was at Bethlehem in the Lehigh Valley, in 1924. I had gone to the place with my publisher, Alfred Knopf, to hear the celebrated Bach Choir, and we were astounded after the first day's sessions to discover that not a drop of malt liquor was to be had in the local pubs. This seemed strange and unfriendly, for it is well known to every musicologist that the divine music of old Johann Sebastian cannot be digested without the aid of its natural solvent. But so far as we could make out there was absolutely none on tap in the Lehigh Valley, though we searched high and low, and threw ourselves upon the mercy of cops, taxi-drivers, hotel clerks, the Elks, the rev. clergy, and half the tenors and basses of the choir. All reported that Prohibition agents had been sighted in the mountains a few days before, and that as a result hundreds of kegs had been buried and every bartender was on the alert. How we got through the second day's sessions I don't know; the music was magnificent, but our tonsils became so parched that we could barely join in the final Amen. Half an hour before our train was scheduled to leave for New York we decided to go down to the Lehigh station and telegraph to a bootician in the big city, desiring him to start westward at once and meet us at Paterson, N. J. On the way to the station we discussed this madcap scheme dismally, and the taxi-driver overheard us. He was a compassionate man, and his heart bled for us.

"Gents," he said, "I hate to horn in on what ain't none of my business, but if you feel that bad about it I think I know where some stuff is to be had. The point is, can you get it?"

We at once offered him money to introduce us, but he waived us off.

"It wouldn't do you no good," he said. "These Pennsylvania Dutch never trust a hackman."

"But where is the place?" we breathed.

"I'm taking you to it," he replied, and in a moment we were there.

It was a huge, blank building that looked like a forsaken warehouse, but over a door that appeared to be tightly locked there was the telltale sign, "Sea Food" — the universal euphemism for beer-house in Maryland and Pennsylvania throughout the thirteen awful years. We rapped on the door and presently it opened about half an inch, revealing an eye and part of a mouth. The ensuing dialogue was *sotto voce* but *staccato* and *appassionata.* The eye saw that we were famished, but the mouth hesitated.

"How do I know," it asked, "that you ain't two of them agents?"

The insinuation made us boil, but we had to be polite.

"*Agents!*" hissed Knopf. "What an idea! Can't you *see* us? Take a good look at us."

The eye looked, but the mouth made no reply.

"Can't you tell musicians when you see them?" I broke in. "Where did you ever see a Prohibition agent who looked so innocent, so moony, so dumb? We are actually fanatics. We came here to hear Bach. Is this the way Bethlehem treats its guests? We came a thousand miles, and now —"

"*Three* thousand miles," corrected Knopf.

"*Five* thousand," I added, making it round numbers.

Suddenly I bethought me that the piano score of the B minor mass had been under my arm all the while. What better introduction? What more persuasive proof of our *bona fides?* I held up the score and pointed to the title on the cover. The eye read:

J. S. Bach
Mass in B Minor

The eye flicked for an instant or two, and then the mouth spoke. " Come in, gents," it said. As the door opened our natural momentum carried us into the bar in one leap, and there we were presently immersed in two immense *Humpen.* The quality we did not pause to observe; what we mainly recalled later was the astounding modesty of the bill, which was sixty-five cents for five *Humpen* — Knopf had two and I had three — and two sandwiches. We made our train just as it was pulling out.

It was a narrow escape from death in the desert, and we do not forget all these years afterward that we owed it to Johann Sebastian Bach, that highly talented and entirely respectable man, and especially to his mass in B minor. In the great city of Cleveland, Ohio, a few months later, I had much worse luck. I went there, in my capacity of newspaper reporter, to help cover the Republican national convention which nominated Calvin Coolidge, and I assumed like everyone else that the Prohibition agents would lay off while the job was put through, if only as a mark of respect to their commander-in-chief. This assumption turned out to be erroneous. The agents actually clamped down on Cleveland with the utmost ferocity, and produced a drought that was virtually complete. Even the local cops and newspaper reporters were dry, and many of the latter spent a large part of their time touring the quarters of the out-of-town correspondents, begging for succor. But the supplies brought in by the correspondents were gone in a few days, and by the time the convention actually opened a glass of malt liquor was as hard to come by in Cleveland as an honest politician.

The news of this horror quickly got about, and one morning I received a dispatch in cipher from a Christian friend in Detroit, saying that he was loading a motor-launch with ten cases of bottled beer and ale, and sending it down the Detroit river and across Lake Erie in charge of two of his goons. They were instructed, he said, to notify me the instant they arrived off the Cleveland breakwater. Their notice reached me the next afternoon, but by that time the boys were nominating Cal, so I could not keep the rendezvous myself, but had to send an agent. This agent was Paul de Kruif, then a young man of thirty-four, studying the literary art under my counsel. Paul was a fellow of high principles and worthy of every confidence; moreover, he was dying of thirst himself. I started him out in a rowboat, and he was gone three hours.

When he got back he was pale and trembling, and I could see at a glance that some calamity had befallen. When he got his breath he gasped out the story.

The two goons, it appeared, had broken into their cargo on the way down from Detroit, for the weather was extremely hot. By the time they anchored off the Cleveland breakwater they had got down three cases, and while they were waiting for de Kruif they knocked off two more. This left but five — and they figured that it was just enough to get them back to Detroit, for the way was uphill all the way, as a glance at a map will show. De Kruif, who was a huge and sturdy Dutchman with a neck like John L. Sullivan, protested violently and even undertook to throw them overboard and pirate the launch and cargo, but they pulled firearms on him, and the best he could do was to get six bottles. These he drank on his return in the rowboat, for the heat, as I have said, was extreme. As a result, I got nothing whatsoever; indeed, not a drop of malt touched my throat until the next night at 11.57, when the express for Washington and points East crossed the frontier of the Maryland Free State.

This was my worst adventure during Prohibition, and in many ways it remains the worst adventure of my whole life, though I have been shot at four times and my travels have taken me to Albania, Trans-Jordan and Arkansas. In Maryland there was always plenty, and when I was in New York Goodman and I made many voyages to Union Hill. One hot night in 1927, while we were lolling in the perfect beerhouse that I have mentioned, a small but excellent band was in attendance, and we learned on inquiry that it belonged to a trans-Atlantic liner of foreign registry, then berthed at one of the North river docks. Through Axel and Raymond we got acquainted with the leader, and he told us that if we cared to accompany him and his men back to the ship they would set up some real Pilsner. We naturally accepted, and at five o'clock the next morning we were still down in the stewards' dining-room on H-deck, pouring in *Seidel* after *Seidel* and victualing royally on black bread and *Leberwurst*. The stewards were scrupulous fellows and would not bootleg, but Goodman had some talent for mathematics, and it was not hard for him to figure out a tip that would cover what we had drunk of their rations, with a reasonable *Zuschlag* added.

Thereafter, we visited that lovely ship every time it was in port, which was about once every five weeks, and in a little while we began to add other ships of the same and allied lines, until in the end we had a whole fleet of them, and had access to Pilsner about three weeks out of four, and not only to Pilsner but also to Münchner, Dortmunder, Würzburger and Kulmbacher. It was a long hoof down the dark pier to the cargo port we had to use, and a long climb from the water-line down to H-deck, but we got used to the exertion and even came to welcome it, for we were both under medical advice to take more exercise. When we went aboard, usually at 10 or 11 p.m., there was no one on the dock save a customs watchman sitting on a stool at the street entrance, chewing tobacco, and when we debarked at 4 or 5 a.m. the same watchman was still there, usually sound asleep.

Gradually, such being the enticements of sin, we fell into the habit of sneaking a couple of jugs past the watchman — most often, of Germany brandy, or *Branntwein.* It was abominable stuff, but nevertheless it was the real McCoy, and Goodman and I found it very useful — he for drugging his actors and I for dishing out to the poets who infested my magazine office. One night there was some sort of celebration aboard ship — as I recall it, the birthday of Martin Luther — and the stewards put on a special spread. The *pièce de résistance* was a *Wurst* of some strange but very toothsome kind, and Goodman and I got down large rashers of it, and praised it in high, astounding terms. The stewards were so pleased by our appreciation that they gave us two whole ones as we left, and so we marched up the pier to the street, each with a bottle of *Branntwein* in one coat pocket and a large, globulous sausage in the other. To our surprise we found the customs watchman awake. More, he halted us.

"What have you got there in your pockets?" he demanded.

We turned them out, and he passed over the two bottles without a word, but the sausages set him off to an amazing snorting and baying.

"God damn me," he roared, "if I ever seen the like. Ain't you got *no* sense *whatever?* Here I try to be nice to you, and let you get something 100% safe into your system, and what do you hand me? What you hand me is that you try to do some *smuggling* on me. Yes, *smuggling*. I know the law and so do you. If I wanted to turn you in I could send you to Atlanta for the rest of your life. God damn if I ain't *ashamed* of you."

With that he grabbed the two sausages and hugged them to him. Goodman and I, conscious of guilt, stood silent, with flushed faces and downcast eyes. What was there to say? Nothing that we could think of. We had been taken red-handed in a deliberate violation of the just laws of this great Republic. We had tried with malice prepense to rob the Treasury of the duty on two valuable sausages — say, 67½ cents at 25% *ad valorem* on a valuation of $2.50 for the pair. The amount, to be sure, was small, but the principle was precious beyond price. In brief, we were common felons, dirt criminals, enemies to society, and as reprehensible, almost, as so many burglars, hijackers or Prohibition agents.

The watchman howled on for two or three minutes, seeking, apparently, to impress upon us the heinousness of our offense. We needed no such exposition. Our consciences were devouring us with red-hot fangs. There was no need for us to say a word, for we radiated repentance and regret. But finally, as the watchman dismissed us with a parting blast, Goodman ventured upon a question.

"Do you," he asked, "want the bottles too?"

"Hell, no," replied the watchman. "What *I* am trying to bust up is *smuggling*."

XVII

INQUISITION

[*1925*]

When I was a *cand. jour.* in the infancy of the century, the old-timer reporters who entertained us youngsters with tales of their professional prodigies (at our expense, of course, for the drinks) always introduced anecdotes of the Johnstown Flood and the march of Coxey's Army. Those were the two great news stories of the last decades of the century just closed, and every reporter with any age and patina on him claimed to have covered them. Most of these caricatures of Richard Harding Davis, I suspect, were liars and no more, but in every considerable city, at least in the East, there must have been plenty who actually saw service on both occasions, for the Johnstown Flood (1889) attracted the largest swarm of journalists ever seen up to that time, and Coxey's Army (1894) had a camp following of them that was almost as large as the army itself. Their narratives, whether true or imaginary, were extremely amusing and instructive to their juniors in the trade, but it didn't take me long to notice that they differed radically in various details, some important and some not. For example, there was not the slightest agreement among them about the authorship of the most famous and enduring literary monument of the flood, to wit, the saying, "Don't spit; remember the Johnstown Flood" — now almost as firmly lodged among American maxims as "It will never get well if you pick it" or "Root, hog, or die." One Polonius laid it to James Creelman, another to Karl Decker, a third to a bartender in Altoona, Pa., a fourth to an office-boy on the New York *Sun*, a fifth to Lew Dockstader, and so on. Nor did they ever agree, even within wide limits, about the number of unfortunates washed into Heaven at Johnstown, or the number of hoboes, runaway boys, three-card monte operators, absconding debtors and other such advanced thinkers who marched with Coxey.

These discrepancies puzzled me at the time, for I was still young and tender, and had not yet learned that neither journalism nor history is an exact science. Since then the fact has been rammed into me by hard experience, and by nothing more effectively than by the Scopes trial at Dayton, Tenn., in 1925, which, as I can prove by both witnesses and documents, I assisted in covering myself. It was, in its way, the Twentieth Century's effort to match the Nineteenth's flood and march. As the reporters who had hands in it always agree when they meet, it had everything — and when they say everything they do not overlook its lack of what is called sex interest, for they know as old hands (they are all fast oxidizing now) that sex interest is not necessary to first-rate drama, as, indeed, the flood and the march proved before them. In another respect, also, it closely resembled those memorable events — that is, in the respect that its saga was quickly embellished with many incidents that never really happened. Before I got home from the scene I was already hearing details that I knew were not true, and more and even less credible ones have been hatching ever since. On the unveracity of one such detail, a small one, I can speak with some authority, for I am a figure in it. It is to the effect that my reports of the trial offended the resident yahoos so grievously that they formed a posse and ran me out of town. This began to get into print soon after the proceedings ended, and the clipping bureaux continue to bring me in new and elaborate forms of it at frequent intervals, even to this day. I have reason to believe that many of the yahoos themselves now accept it as true, and that there are heroes among them who claim to have been members of the posse, and to have taken pot shots at me as I ran screaming down the road.

Nothing of the sort ever happened. It is a fact that my dispatches from the courtroom were somewhat displeasing to local susceptibilities, and that my attempts to describe the town and its people were even more so, and it is also a fact that there was talk among certain bolder spirits of asking me to retire from the scene, but beyond that it did not go. So far as I can recall, only one Daytonian ever went to the length of opening the subject to me, and he was extremely polite. He was one of the catchpolls of the court, and all he had to say was that there was some murmuring against me, and that he thought it might be a good idea if I met a few of the principal citizens and let them tell me precisely what was complained of in my writings. I could see no objection to that, and accordingly offered to meet these notables at the drugstore — the Acropolis and Mars' Hill of the town — the same evening. I got there on time and so did the catchpoll, but a heavy thunderstorm was making up, and the rest of the committee failed to appear. So the catchpoll and I, after waiting half an hour, parted amicably, and that was the last I heard of the matter. I was in Dayton for at least four or five days longer, carrying on my work without the slightest molestation, and when I left at last — unhappily, before the butchery of Bryan by Clarence Darrow — it was at a time chosen before I came, and at my own sole volition. Some of the other reporters present, hearing of the murmuring aforesaid and eager to begaud the lily of the trial with gilding, professed to take the posse seriously, and let it be known that they were organizing a counter-posse of their own, with Lindsay Denison of the New York *World* as its commander. Inasmuch as there were nearly 200 reporters in the place, many of them veterans of riots, lynchings, torch murders and labor wars, it may be that the Daytonians took this counter-posse seriously and were induced thereby to cool off, but if so I certainly have no evidence of it. All I can report is that they treated me with great courtesy, despite the necessary unpleasantness of my reports, and that five years later, when the William Jennings Bryan Fundamentalist " University " was set up in a cow pasture adjoining the town, I was invited to attend its consecration, and it was even hinted that I might be allowed to make a speech.

The only strangers who actually suffered any menace to their lives and limbs during the progress of the trial were Clarence Darrow, the chief lawyer for Scopes; William K. Hutchinson of the Hearst papers; an unknown Y.M.C.A. secretary who wandered in from Cincinnati, and an itinerant atheist who came to town to exhibit a mangy chimpanzee. All four were threatened, not with assassination nor even with tarring-and-feathering, but simply with confinement in the town hoosegow; but inasmuch as the hoosegow was a one-room brick pillbox set in the middle of an open field, and the average noonday temperature in the valley of the Tennessee river during July, 1925 was at least 100 degrees, this amounted virtually to capital punishment. Only the atheist and the Y.M.C.A. brother ever got into that dreadful cooler, but the other two made narrow escapes. Hutchinson, in fact, appeared to be doomed, but at the last minute he was rescued by the magnificent forensic powers of Richard J. Beamish, then of the Philadelphia *Inquirer* and now a high dignitary in the Pennsylvania State government, with the rank and pay of a lieutenant-general. The crime of Hutch, a very competent and resourceful reporter, was that he had outsmarted the learned judge on the bench, a village Hampden named Raulston. The lawyers for Scopes — Darrow, Arthur Garfield Hays, Dudley Field Malone and John T. Neal — had made the usual formal motion to quash the indictment, and the judge, with a great show of judicial dog, announced that he would ponder his decision. He kept on pondering it so long that everyone ran out of patience, and various efforts were made to pump him, but it remained for Hutch to do the trick. He worked it by the simple device of asking the judge if, after the decision was given, the court would adjourn until the next day. The judge replied that it would, and Hutch had his secret, for if the decision sustained the motion to quash, the trial would be at an end and there would be no next day. Within ten minutes the Hearst papers had a flash saying that the indictment would be sustained, and so they beat the country. And within half an hour the representatives of all the super- and infra-Hearst papers began to receive remonstrances from their home offices, and were clustered around the judge like bees in full fermentation, demanding to know why he had given the beat to Hutch.

This upbraiding greatly upset His Honor, and also puzzled him sorely. He realized in his dim, judicial way that he had been had, but he couldn't make out how. He tried to solve the problem by a two-headed device. First, he ordered the whole corps of correspondents herded into his courtroom for an inquiry *en masse*, and second, he cited Hutch for contempt of court. Many of the non-Hearst correspondents were inflamed against Hutch for beating them so neatly, but when they began to think of the possible consequences of the charge he faced — say, thirty days in that red-hot coop of a can in the field behind the courthouse — their sense of brotherhood overcame their ire, and they tried to devise ways and means to save him. In this Christian work the leadership was soon taken by Dick Beamish. Rising in court in his most impressive manner, he made a speech saying that the matter at issue was full of vexation, and had given all the more seasoned correspondents great perturbation. Not only were grave questions of law involved, but also questions of journalistic ethics. It might very well be — who could say offhand? — that Hutch was guilty not only of violating the statutes of Tennessee but also of shaming the great profession he theoretically adorned. There was, in Maître Beamish's judgment, but one way to get to the bottom of the matter, and that was to appoint a committee of distinguished reporters to consider all its bearings and report upon them at length. The judge fell for this, and at once appointed a committee with Beamish as its chairman. The other members were Phil Kinsley of the Chicago *Tribune*, Forrest Davis of the New York *Herald Tribune*, Earl Shaub of the Universal Service, and Tony Muto, a free lance weighing 260 pounds.

This committee was in session all night in Beamish's quarters over the town hay, feed, lime and cement store. It appointed Lindsay Denison its sheriff, and from time to time he dragged in some elder correspondent to act as *amicus curiae*. I was the only reporter on hand who had any public standing as a moral theologian, but Beamish categorically forbade Denison to summon me — a lamentable evidence that the old feud between the civil and the canon law, running back to the Eleventh Century, was still running. The deliberations of the committee, of course, were secret, but with so many outsiders going in and coming out some notion of their drift reached the gallery. At the precise stroke of midnight, it appeared, Tony Muto drew a royal flush, and half an hour later Phil Kinsley, a great believer in bold experiment, drew four aces to a nine. As the laboring of legal and ethical points grew more and more animated even greater marvels were witnessed. There was, so we were told, one hand of five kings and another of six (some said seven) queens. Beamish was broke and in hock for $7 by 2.30 a.m., but toward dawn he made a glorious recovery, partly due to luck and partly to science, and when the committee, having finished its deliberations, rose at 6 a.m. he was solvent again. So, in fact, were all the others. Only one of them, Muto, was appreciably ahead of the game, and he was ahead to the extent of no more than $3 or $4. Their work done, the committeemen shaved with Beamish's razor, bathed in a washtub, and entered the hay for a brief snooze before reporting to Raulston, J. When His Honor rapped for order at 10 a.m. they were lined up respectfully before his bar, headed by their chairman and spokesman.

The whole course of the trial of Scopes was marked by gorgeous oratory, and I shall make note of another specimen of it anon, but from end to end I heard nothing more magnificent than Beamish's report. He was then at the height of his powers as a rhetorician, and in addition he was a very fine figure of a man, with broad shoulders, an attention-compelling but symmetrical paunch, and a very cocky way of carrying his head. It was the fashion of the time to wear shirts of somewhat loud design, and he had the loudest in Dayton. They were of printed silk, and ran to all the colors of the rainbow, along with many aniline inventions that no rainbow since Noah's time had ever boasted. The public admired them and Beamish loved them so tenderly that he had affectionate names for some of them — the Garden of Allah, Who is Sylvia?, the Dark-Brown Taste, I'm Called Little Buttercup, the Apotheosis of the Rose, and so on. For his effort in behalf of poor Hutch he chose the queen of his sartorial harem — a superb polychrome creation called Everybody's Sweetheart. Nobody wore coats in Dayton, so the crowd in the courtroom got a sizzling eyeful when he arose. But in half a minute the roll of his sonorous periods made everyone forget his splendors, and the whole audience, including the lawyers and the learned judge, was bedazzled and enchanted by the surge and thunder of his words.

So far as I know, no stenographic report of his speech was made, and I shall not attempt to recall it in any detail, for its effectiveness depended quite as much on manner as on content. It included, I remember clearly enough, a review of the struggle for free speech in the Anglo-Saxon countries since Beowulf's time, with extracts from the Areopagitica, the evidence and arguments in the trial of John Peter Zenger, and the writings of John Stuart Mill. There were citations, first and last, of at least a hundred cases — some of them from the standard English and American reports, but a number dredged up from obscure proceedings before county judges and police magistrates in such States as Arkansas, Idaho and Vermont — most of them unknown to the books and maybe also to history. The judge listened eagerly, and no wonder, for it is highly improbable that any argument of the same scope, punch and profundity had ever been offered in his court, or indeed in any other court of Tennessee. At length the sough of words ceased, and Beamish paused to mop his brow, hitch up his pants, fleck a horse-fly off the left arm of Everybody's Sweetheart, and intone the recommendation of the committee. His voice was now low and caressing, and as he came to the end he took a statuesque stance, adjusted his Oxford *pince-nez* on the end of his nose, threw back his head, and looked *under* the horn-rimmed lenses at the judge. "And therefore, Your Honor," he concluded, "your committee, having considered all the facts in a fair and impartial spirit, and given deep and prolonged thought to the questions of journalistic ethics that appear to be involved, now recommends most respectfully that no further proceedings be had." "It is so ordered!" exclaimed the judge, with a loud bang of his gavel, and thus Bill Hutchinson escaped the cooler, and the trial of the infidel Scopes was resumed.

Scopes himself, a modest and good-looking young man, was quickly overshadowed by the eminent characters who heaved and howled in the courtroom — Bryan, Darrow, Hays, Malone and so on. Once, after he had been unseen and unheard for two or three days, the judge stopped the proceedings to inquire what had become of him. He was found — in his shirtsleeves like everyone else — sitting in the middle of a dense mass of lawyers, infidels, theologians, biologists and reporters, and after he had risen and identified himself the uproar was resumed. Darrow, who wore wide firemen's suspenders and had a trick of running his arms under them as he spoke, was threatened with the hoosegow out in the field for a chance remark during one of his interminable arguments. The judge, sweating under his logic, which was couched in somewhat bellicose terms, stopped him and observed: "I hope counsel does not intend any offense to this court." Darrow thereupon paused, yawned ostentatiously, flapped his suspenders a couple of times, and answered: "Your Honor is at least entitled to hope." This brought down the judicial gavel with a thwack that shook the courtroom, and ten seconds later the trial was suspended and Darrow was before the bar to answer a charge of contempt of court. He naturally asked for a chance to consult his associates, and there was a wait while they put their heads together. In the end they decided that the easiest way out was for him to apologize, and this he did in extremely grudging words, with his voice full of stealthy sneers. But the letter of the apology was there, and the judge accepted it without further ado.

The atheist who suffered in the town calaboose was a traveling showman who had wandered in with his chimpanzee to make propaganda for Darwin. He parked it at the railroad station, which was near the jail, and went through the town distributing inflammatory circulars. Their purport was that his chimpanzee proved to the eye, and with irrefutable force, that man and the higher apes were identical, and that a peek at it for the small sum of ten cents, along with the accompanying lecture by the atheist himself, would convince any reasonable customer, however pious. The days of Genesis, according to the circular, were pretty well over. As soon as every man, woman and child had seen the chimpanzee and noted its striking resemblance to a United States Senator, the American people would rise in a body and chase all their ordained pastors from their settlements. The atheist was a mild man, and his chimpanzee appeared to be at the point of death, but his selling talk aroused the local Fundamentalists, and in a little while he was clapped into jail. When Denison and I heard of this we went to the proper authorities, and demanded to see the chapter and verse of the Tennessee statute under which he was held. There was, of course, no such statute. The law that Scopes had run afoul of prohibited teaching Darwinism to children in the public schools, not to adults outside. But the authorities argued that they had general powers to put down any and every act in contempt of the revelation of God, and we had a dreadful time convincing them that caging the atheist in that furnace out in the field was cruel and unusual punishment. Finally, they compromised by agreeing to transfer him to a small hotel down at the railroad station, on condition that he would leave by the first outbound train, taking his obscene and sclerotic ape with him. There was a wait of three hours until the next train left, and the atheist gave them over to throwing copies of his circulars out of his second-floor window. A sort of vigilance committee was formed to gather up these circulars as they fluttered down, and burn them before they could fall into the hands of the young. But a number escaped, and they are still preserved, I hear, in the less pious sort of Tennessee Valley homes, in secret cupboards which also house jugs of forty-rod, pictures of naked women, and birth-control apparatus.

The Y.M.C.A. brother got into trouble as a result of an oafish pleasantry by my colleague, Henry M. Hyde, and myself, no doubt in bad taste. On our first day in Dayton we had gone about scraping acquaintance with the country evangelists who were swarming into town, and among them we were especially delighted by an old man named T. T. Martin, hailing from Blue Mountain, Miss. This Brother Martin, a white haired commissar of Yahweh in a clerical black coat and a collar so wide that he could pull his head through it, was a fellow full of Christian juices, and amiable to believer and infidel alike. He was one of the recognized stars of his profession, and had accumulated enough " plant," as he called it, to load two trucks. It consisted of a large stock of dog's-eared Bibles, another of hymnbooks, a reed organ of powerful voice, a portable pulpit, and a set of knock-down bleachers like those used by a one-ring circus. These bleachers he set up on the courthouse lawn, and there he not only used them at his own services but also lent them freely to rival John Baptists. He made a gallant effort to save the abandoned souls of Hyde and me, and would take a hack at us every time he met us on the streets, which was ten or twenty times a day. Indeed, he continued these efforts by mail long after the Scopes trial was over, and when he died at last, only a few years ago, he was full of friendly hopes that the seed he had jabbed into us would fructify soon or late, and that he would thus have the pleasure of meeting us in Heaven with his rings in our ears.

One morning, on meeting him in front of the town drugstore, we sought to get rid of his solicitations by hinting that important news was astir. What was it? We hemmed and hawed a bit, and then told him that it was a report from Cincinnati that a gang of Bolsheviki there were planning to come down to Dayton and butcher Bryan. At that time the Red scare following World War I was still in full blast, and in consequence Brother Martin was considerably perturbed. We warned him to keep his mouth shut, but when we left him he rushed off to the house where Bryan was staying and gave the alarm. The result was that the town constables got into a panic, and sent a hurry call for help to Chattanooga. An hour later thirty or forty Chattanooga cops got in, and the lieutenant in charge of them threw them in a cordon around Dayton, to challenge all suspicious persons as they approached. An extra heavy force was posted at the railroad station, where the afternoon express from Cincinnati was due in a little while. When it arrived only one passenger alighted — the Y.M.C.A. brother aforesaid. He looked innocent enough, God knows, for he wore a black cutaway coat and (despite the infernal heat) a high choker collar, and carried a Bible under his arm. But the Chattanooga cops were taking no chances, so they grabbed him as he alighted and rushed him to the hoosegow. There he sweated and bellowed for an hour while Hyde and I (whose consciences had begun to fever us) joined Brother Martin in trying to convince the cops that he was really what he said he was, and not a Russian trigger-man of democracy. In the end the cops let him go, but not until his choker collar was a ring of mush. He got another one somewhere, and that night he delivered a vociferous tirade against Bolshevism, boozing, atheism and their allied infamies from Brother Martin's collapsible tabernacle on the courthouse lawn. Brother Martin had forgotten where he got the tip about the attempt on Bryan even before he reached Bryan's quarters, panting and half scared to death. An hour later, in fact, when Hyde and I met him again, he imparted it to us as news, and we thanked him very politely.

Bryan, of course, was the star of the show, and when he appeared upon the streets, always in his shirtsleeves and wearing a curious deep-collared shirt made for him by his wife, he was followed by a large gallery of the local Bible searchers. Many tackled him with problems of exegesis that had floored them in their studies, but he never lacked a prompt and convincing answer. Now and then a Holy Roller, a Dunkard, a Unitarian or even a downright infidel had at him with a trick question, but he always turned them off facilely, for he was as thoroughly soaked in the Holy Scriptures as many another aspirant to the Presidency has been in alcohol. Bryan liked country people, and was at ease among them. Whenever he encountered a mountain family from the Pamirs behind Dayton, the husband and father in his go-to-meeting overalls, the wife and mother giving titty (as the local phrase had it) to her youngest child, and the rest peeking from behind her skirts, he would stop his parade long enough to greet them with the courtly deportment he had picked up from the Spanish ambassador during his days as Secretary of State. This ceremonious greeting always made a powerful impression upon the assembled hinds. There were many among them who believed that Bryan was no longer merely human, but had lifted himself to some level or other of the celestial angels, archangels, principalities, powers, virtues, dominations, thrones, cherubim and seraphim. It would have surprised no one if he had suddenly begun to perform miracles — say, curing a mule of heaves or a yokel of kidney weakness, or striking oil in the field behind the courthouse. I saw plenty of his customers approach him stealthily to touch his garments, to wit, his shirt and pants. Those with whom he shook hands were made men, and not a few of them, I daresay, are showing the marks on their palms to this day. If the Protestant theologies prevailing in Appalachia did not prohibit relics as heathenish, every church in the whole region would have some souvenir of him under its high altar, if only a lock of hair, a lead pencil or a page from one of his battery of Bibles.

That the Tennessee of 1925 was still in the Age of Miracles was proved to me by a curious personal experience. Before I left for the Scopes trial I had a session in New York with Edgar Lee Masters, a merry fellow who delights in poking fun at the common faiths and superstitions of the country, often by means of burlesque handbills. He told me that, if I would agree to distribute it at Dayton, he'd prepare such a handbill in the name of one of his favorite stooges, an imaginary evangelist named the Rev. Elmer Chubb, LL.D., D.D. I agreed of course, and a day or two before I set out I received about 1,000 copies of the following:

COMING! COMING!

TO DAYTON, TENNESSEE

During the Trial of the Infidel Scopes

ELMER CHUBB, LL.D., D.D.

FUNDAMENTALIST AND MIRACLE WORKER

MIRACLES PERFORMED ON THE PUBLIC SQUARE!

Dr. Chubb will allow himself to be bitten by any poisonous snake, scorpion, gila monster, or other reptile. He will also drink any poison brought to him. . . . In demonstration of the words of our Lord and Saviour Jesus Christ, as found in the 16th Chapter of the Gospel of St. Mark:

> *"And these signs shall follow them that believe: in my name shall they cast out devils, they shall speak with new tongues; they shall take up serpents, and if they drink any deadly thing it shall in no wise hurt them; they shall lay hands on the sick and they shall recover."*

PUBLIC DEMONSTRATION of healing, casting out devils, and prophesying. Dr. Chubb will also preach in Aramaic, Hebrew, Greek, Latin, Coptic, Egyptian, and in the lost languages of the Etruscans and the Hittites.

TESTIMONIALS – *all favorable but one:*

With my own eyes I saw Dr. Chubb swallow cyanide of potassium. WILLIAM JENNINGS BRYAN, CHRISTIAN STATESMAN

Dr. Chubb simply believes the word of God, and his power follows. REV. J. FRANK NORRIS

I was possessed of devils, and Dr. Chubb cast them out of me. Glory to God. MAGDALENA RAYBACK, R.F.D. 3, DUNCAN GROVE, MICH.

When under the spell of divine inspiration Dr. Chubb speaks Coptic as fluently as if it were his mother tongue. As to Etruscan, I cannot say. PROF. ADDISON BLAKESLEY.

Chubb is a fake. I can mix a cyanide cocktail that will make him turn up his toes in thirty seconds. H. L. MENCKEN

SPECIAL NOTICE: Dr. Chubb has never pretended that he had power to raise the dead. The Bible shows that only the Saviour and Twelve Apostles had that power.

Free will offering, dedicated to the enforcement of the anti-evolution laws.

When the trial got under way I hired a couple of boys to distribute these circulars, and that night Henry Hyde and I went to the courthouse green to see what would turn up. Precisely nothing turned up. Hundreds of copies of the circulars were flying about the grass, and dozens of yokels had them in their hands, but no one showed any interest in Dr. Elmer Chubb. A few discreet inquiries told us why. It was that the miracles he offered were old stuff in upland Tennessee. Nearly every one of the evangelists roaring at that moment was ready to undertake at least some of them, and there were other evangelists back in the hills who offered to do them all. A few nights later we saw and heard some of the latter at a Holy Roller camp five or six miles from Dayton: it was patronized by yahoos who believed that Dayton itself was so full of sin that they refused to enter it, even to see Bryan. To be sure, the performers we saw confined themselves mainly to speaking in the tongues, and did not venture to drink poison or to let snakes bite them, but only a little while later they proceeded to both operations, and after half a dozen of them had been floored the State police closed in on them, Mark or no Mark. But they resisted stoutly, and their customers with them, and during the eight or ten years following the infidel Northern newspapers reported a great many unhappy failures of the magic, some of them fatal. The question whether the effort to put them down was or was not in contempt of Divine Revelation became a political issue in Tennessee, with all the principal statesmen of the State sweating to take up a safe middle position, as they had at the time of the Scopes trial.

So far as I can recall, Bryan never expressed any public opinion on the subject, but his frequent declaration that every word in the King James Bible was literally true, including the typographical errors, ranged him on the side of the wonder-workers, and they were all hot for him. For Darrow they naturally had no taste, not only because he derided the Good Book, but also and principally because they really believed in miracles, and were confident that Jahveh would fetch him soon or late. Thus they kept away from him, for they didn't want to be present when the lightnings from Heaven began to fall. Their customers shared this fear, and it went so far that whenever a thunderstorm blew up, which was very often in that tropical weather, everyone save a few atheists began to edge away from Darrow in the courtroom. On the street, when the skies were clear, he had followers like Bryan, but they were by no means so numerous and most of them kept at a prudent distance. Once a mule ran away on the main street, and the whole crowd took to its heels, convinced by the clatter that Darrow's time had come. Bryan was gorged and stuffed at colossal country meals by all the surrounding gentry and illuminati, but old Clarence had to mess miserably with Hays and Malone.

Both of these juniors were also regarded as doomed, but it was generally believed that Darrow would be knocked off first, so the bolder spirits sometimes approached them quite closely, especially when no thunderstorm was in prospect. Here Malone's Irish blarney also came into effect, for he could talk even a Tennessee Baptist into smiling on him. On one horrible occasion, in fact, he came near talking the yokel jury into acquitting Scopes.

This, of course, was not to the taste of Darrow, for he was shrewd enough to see that if the prisoner in the box were acquitted the case would soon be forgotten, including even Bryan's part in it. Inasmuch as his main aim in defending Scopes was to plaster Bryan before the country as a jackass, he hoped that his ostensible client would be condemned to the hulks, for that would enable him to appeal to the Supreme Court of Tennessee, and maybe even to the Supreme Court of the United States, and so keep the searing spotlight upon Bryan. Thus he was dreadfully disconcerted one afternoon when Malone launched into a speech so eloquent that in five minutes the jurymen were visibly wobbling, and in ten minutes even the learned judge was beginning to gulp, pant and scratch himself. The subject of the speech was some formal motion of no importance, and after sending in Malone to do the job Darrow relaxed into his firemen's suspenders and prepared for a quiet little snooze. But he got no snooze that day, for Malone leaped into it with all the fervor of an Irishman pulling the British lion's tail. As I have said, the Daytonians were (and, I suppose, still are) great fans for rhetoric, and they were presently getting a horse-doctor's dose of it. Malone began no louder than an auctioneer crying a sale, but in a few minutes he let his larynx have the gas, and thereafter he produced such blasts and hurricanes of sound that I never heard the like of them until I encountered Gerald L. K. Smith eleven years later. Let him come to the end of a sentence on an open vowel, and it sounded like the roar of a thousand massed lions. Let him stop upon a consonant, and the effect was that of smashing a hundred tons of crockery. There was no loud-speaker in the courtroom, but Dudley did not need it. With his own naked voice he filled the big room with so vast and terrifying a din that it seemed almost to bulge the walls. The yaps could not make out the drift of his remarks, but they were charmed by his execution. Sitting beside Darrow in the lawyers' pen, I watched them as the poison ran through them. First they sat up, then their eyes began to sparkle, and then they half rose from their chairs and fell to breathing heavily. In a little while they were breaking into cheers at the end of every sentence, and some of the more ebullient of them were leaping up and howling. The jurymen went the same way, and even the learned judge, as I have said, began to show signs of succumbing.

All this, of course, was very disturbing to Darrow. "Great God!" he whispered to me; "the scoundrel will hang the jury!" Thereupon he began to make frantic signals to Malone, commanding him to desist, but Malone, like any other orator, was so intoxicated by the exuberance of his own verbosity that he was deaf, dumb and blind. Indeed, if lightning had struck Darrow at that minute he'd have missed it. The one hope was that he would run out of breath soon or late, but for a while he seemed to be fetching up all that he needed, and more. But in the end, of course, his lungs began to creak and splatter, and finally, after a series of cyclonic gasps that first made his face a bright red and then left it dead white, he shut down at last and staggered out for air. One of his hearers had been his charming wife, Doris Stevens; she was standing in a corner of the courtroom surrounded by a group of Army officers who had come up from a nearby camp for the day's show. Dudley made for her with the sure instinct of any husband, and she proceeded to mop and soothe him as in wifely duty bound. I left Darrow and followed along, eager to offer my felicitations on what was undoubtedly the loudest speech ever delivered by mortal man since Apostolic times. The Army officers crowded up to be introduced to the orator and his wife, and it fell to me to present them. Doris, in those days, was a violent Lucy Stoner, and had been denouncing the reporters every time they addressed her or wrote of her as Mrs. Malone. But while the delighted anthropoids still roared their applause I bethought me of the first eight verses of Ecclesiastes III, so I approached the lady's ear and whispered: "What is it to be, Doris? Miss Stevens or Mrs. Malone?" Stroking her husband's glistening bald head, she blushed prettily and answered: "Let it be Mrs. Malone — this time." So when I presented the Army officers to her it was in the character of a bourgeois wife. Her husband, under her ministrations, recovered quickly, and that evening after dinner he took Hays for $17 with four nines.

XVIII

VANISHING ACT

[*1934*]

Taking one day with another I have but little hankering to see ruins, but when, in the early part of 1934, I found myself aboard a ship approaching the French port of Tunis, in the Mediterranean, and a Catholic bishop who was a fellow-passenger proposed that we go ashore the next day and have a look at the remains of Carthage I agreed at once, for the Carthaginians have always fascinated me, if only because they made so thorough a job of disappearing from the earth. His Excellency, it appeared, was but little interested in them himself, for they were heathens as I was, and hence outside his ordinary jurisdiction; what made him want to see their capital was simply the fact that the Roman city built upon its site had been the stamping-ground of the celebrated Tertullian, who wrote his "Apologeticus" there, and a frequent resort of the even more renowned and much less dubious St.

Augustine. The actual see of Augustine, however, was not Carthage but Hippo, and the bishop and I put in a couple of hours trying to find out where Hippo was, for if it was nearby we might very well make a side trip to it. Unhappily, none of the guide-books in the ship's library threw any light on the question, and we had about given it up as unanswerable when we happened upon a dog's-eared German encyclopedia and learned from it that there were actually two Hippos, both of them to the west of Carthage. The first, it appeared, was still carried on the books of the Vatican as Hippo Diarrhytus and the second as Hippo Regius, but now they were only the theoretical cathedral towns of titular dioceses, without anything in them even remotely resembling cathedrals. If they actually had bishops then those bishops had probably never seen them, nor made any serious inquiries into their spiritual condition, but were engaged instead upon paper work at Rome. Which Hippo was Augustine's? The encyclopedia was not altogether clear on the point, but we concluded after some speculation (as it turned out, rightly) that it must be Hippo Regius, and dug up an atlas to find out where it lay. There was no such town in the atlas, and it was not until we landed at Tunis the next day that we learned that Hippo Regius had changed its name to Bône, and was so far from Tunis that getting there and back would take us three or four days. So we gave up the idea of visiting the see of Augustine, and contented ourselves with taking a look at Carthage.

What is left of it, we found, lies about ten miles northeast of the city of Tunis, on the brow of a little hill now called Byrsa, jutting out into the Gulf of Tunis, with the blue of the Mediterranean fading off into the distance beyond. The slope of the hill is steep in front, and the pea-green inshore waters of the gulf come quite close to the site, but on the landward side the descent is gradual, and vague farms that seem almost level show themselves now and again through the dust of the Tunisian plain. There is an automobile road up from Tunis, and also a trolley line that stops at the foot of the hill. Down on the beach a few fishermen haul in their nets, and in the other direction balls of denser dust show where some laborious husbandman is plowing with donkey or camel. The landscape looks almost as peaceful as that of Iowa. There is no quick movement in it, not even from birds, and the ear catches no sound. Yet it has seen some of the wildest fighting ever recorded, and the climaxes of that fighting were almost always massacres. The earliest navigators of the Mediterranean, coming probably from Crete, fought for a toe-hold on the shore against the primeval anthropophagi, and then against one another for the trade that, even in those remote days, flowed up to the gulf from the black abysm of Africa. By the Ninth Century B.C. the Phoenicians, who were the English of the ancient world, had driven out all the rest and built a handsome *cart hadash,* or new town, on the bluff, and by the Third Century it was greater than Tyre, their capital, and its sailors and traders roved all the waters from Syria to the Pillars of Hercules, and even beyond. There is, indeed, every reason to believe that they circumnavigated Africa at least 1,800 years before Vasco da Gama. The chief port of this Western trade was always Carthage. From it radiated routes that reached to the farthest frontiers of the known world. The Carthaginians controlled the sea-borne carrying trade of that world, and were its greatest jobbers and bankers, and whenever they found a good harbor they set up a colony, and reached out from it for the business of the back country. One of those colonies, Tarshish in Spain, was so prosperous that it became, in Biblical times, a sort of common symbol of opulence. Also, it became a refuge for the broken and outlawed men of the whole Mediterranean littoral, and it was there that Jonah tried to hide himself when he got into trouble with Jahveh, as your pastor will tell you. But today Tarshish is only a measly fishing village at the mouth of the Guadalquiver, bearing about the same relation to Cadiz that Sagaponack, L. I., does to New York. As for Carthage itself, it is not even a village, but only a spot.

Certainly there must be few parallels in history to the completeness of its destruction. The Romans, like all the other Japs and Nazis of antiquity, threw their hearts into the job when they undertook to pull an enemy town to pieces, but there is no record that they ever went so far anywhere else as at Carthage. Consider, for example, the kindred case of Jerusalem, destroyed in the year 70 A.D. That was an earnest and comprehensive piece of work, as such things go, and the Jews still wail it as their worst disaster since the Babylonian Captivity; but let us not forget that the wall before which they do their wailing survived the Roman mortars and torpedo-bombs almost undamaged, and remains in excellent repair to this day. Nor is it the only healthy relic of the days before Jerusalem was hypothetically wiped out, to rise no more; the town, in fact, is full of odds and ends that are ascribed, at least by the guides, to the ages of Solomon, Moses, Abraham and even Adam. But at Carthage the Romans really spit on their hands, and in consequence the remains of the city, once so rich and so puissant, are no greater in bulk and hardly greater in significance than the remains of a barn struck by lightning. The French fathers settled in the place have raked up everything they could find and stored it in what they call a museum, but you could get the whole contents of that museum into a couple of boxcars, and most of them are mere scraps and potsherds, unidentified and unidentifiable. For when the Romans demolished Carthage they not only tore down and removed all its buildings, and plowed up its streets, and filled its wells, and emptied its graves; they also devoured and annihilated all its records, so that what is known about it today, save for the major outlines of its history, is next to nothing. Of its people we have only a few names — Hannibal, Hamilcar and so on, nearly all of them of military men. The one Carthaginian author who is remembered is Sanchuniathon, and he is remembered only because a fifth-rate Greek once mentioned him, and probably also invented him.

The bishop and I were through with the relics in half an hour, and when we had finished we were no wiser than we had been before. What use did the Carthaginians make of the little stone boxes that were stretched out in a meagre row? The prevailing theory is that they were coffins for the ashes of children sacrificed to the national god, who is assumed to have been the Phoenician Moloch, but that is only a guess, and for all anyone knows to the contrary the name of the god may have been Goldberg or McGinnis, and the creatures sacrificed to him may have been, not children at all, but dogs, cats or goats. If he had a temple that temple is now less than dust, and if it had priests then all the gold, silver, myrrh and frankincense accumulated by those priests is now the same. Even the new town that the Romans built on the site long after the old one was destroyed is far along the road to annihilation and forgetfulness. Its best preserved relic is the shell of a theatre — now greatly resembling a stone quarry in the last stages of bankruptcy and decay. While His Excellency and I contemplated what is left of it, some boys who were passengers in our ship recreated themselves by leaping up and down its moldering tiers. Presently one of these boys missed his step and skinned his shins, and under cover of his caterwauling we withdrew. There was an Englishman nearby engaged upon a lecture to such visitors as cared to hear him. We listened for a while and found his patter far superior to that of the average guide, but what he had to say was, after all, precisely nothing, and that was what we already knew.

So we moved away to a quiet place overlooking the dusty Tunisian plain, and fell into silent pondering, each on his own. I can't tell you what form the bishop's meditations took, for high ecclesiastics are not given to confidences in that field, but my own, I recall, dwelt altogether on the complete obliteration, not only of Carthage the town, but also of its people. They were, I have no doubt, divided into groups and moieties as we are today, and showed all the sharp differences of fortune, virtue, capacity and opinion that have marked human societies at all times and everywhere. There must have been Carthaginians who were admired and envied by the rest, and other Carthaginians who were envied and disliked. Whenever a new source of cocoanuts, ivory or ebony was discovered along the African coast, or a new tin mine in Cornwall, or a new fishing bank in the waters to the North, there must have been a heavy inflow of fresh money, and a large part of that fresh money, you may be sure, was collared by individual Carthaginians of superior smartness, and laid out in ostentations of the sort that win public respect and lay the foundations of doggy families. It is not hard to imagine what followed, for the same thing is going on today, not only in all the great nations of Christendom, but also in the black kingdoms of the African jungle and the barbarisms of Inner Asia. Once Father had the money the rest followed almost automatically. If there were any daughters in the family the general estimation of their pulchritude went up by 200 or 300%, and all save the one who fell in love with a lieutenant in the army made elegant and even gaudy marriages — maybe with the sons of old families that traced their ancestry back to the motherland of Phoenicia and claimed descent from a Duke of Byblus or Zarephath; maybe even with some actual member of the Phoenician nobility, sent out to the colonies to recoup the failing fortunes of his house. As for the sons of the new plutocrat, they went through the Harvard of the time (first missing Groton, but making Lawrenceville), put in five or six years playing polo and keeping dancing women, and then married soberly and settled down to sitting on boards of directors, serving as vestrymen of the temple of Moloch (or

Goldberg, or McGinnis), and waiting patiently for the exitus of their now venerable pa.

By the time he shuffled off at last, leaving doctors' bills to the amount of at least a ton of gold, they were fathers themselves, with wives growing bulky and pious, daughters who never had enough clothes, and sons who broke the legs of the family elephants playing polo and had to be ransomed ever and anon from the clutches of designing wenches from Crete, Sicily and Spain. The grandchildren continued the sempiternal and inevitable round, familiar in Sumer and still familiar in this great free republic. Some of them, born idiots, became philosophers and refused to bathe. Others went in for gambling and were soon in hock to their brothers and cousins. Others succumbed to the evangelists of new religions who were constantly coming in from the eastward, and went about arguing that Moloch (or Goldberg, or McGinnis) was really not a god at all, but only the emanation of a god, and that his parent divinity was someone of the same name, or some other name, in Mesopotamia, the Hittite country, or elsewhere. Yet others laid out their heritage backing schemers who claimed to have discovered tin mines in Carthage itself, not twenty miles from the City Hall; or assembled vast collections of unintelligible papyri from the upper Nile, and employed Greeks with long whiskers to catalogue them; or bought large ranches in the hinterland and undertook to raise elephants, camels or giraffes; or organized gangs of gladiators and took them along the North African coast, challenging all comers; or drove chariots down the main street to the peril of the cops, street-sweeps, blind men and school children, and landed finally in the sanitarium on the mountain over behind what is now Tunis. The fourth generation produced a high percentage of whores and drunkards, and began to slip back to the primordial nonentity. Some of the cadets of the younger lines enlisted in the army, or in the Phoenician Foreign Legion, and were killed fighting Assyrians, Persians, Greeks or Romans. Others became policemen, bookkeepers, sailors, collectors for the orphans, *schochets* or *mohels* (for the Carthaginians were Semitic), school teachers, fortune tellers, barbers, priests, stone masons or horse doctors, or even garbage haulers, fish pedlars or jail wardens. But not infrequently there was at least one line that kept its money and held up its collective head, and after a century or two it came to be accepted as ancient and eminent, and began to look down its nose at the rest of the people. The gradual accumulation of such lines produced an aristocracy — an inevitable phenomenon in human society, then as now. That aristocracy had arisen from the trading class, but in the end it was clearly and admittedly superior to the trading class. Its members were regarded with deference by the commonalty, and had a long list of special opportunities and privileges. One of its constituent families, in the later days of Carthage, was that of Hannibal and Hamilcar.

But that it actually ruled the country is not very probable, for aristocracies, taking one century with another, are hardly more than false-faces. They sit in the parlor, so to speak, but down in the boiler-room quite different gangs are at work. Those gangs, whatever the form of government, are composed of professional governors, which is to say, of politicians, orators, intriguers, demagogues. They commonly occupy, in the hierarchy of caste, a place below the salt, and it is unusual for them to transmit their talents and power to their descendants, but while they last all real power is in their hands, whether the country they infest be a monarchy, an oligarchy or a free republic. As I have said, we know next to nothing of the internal history of Carthage, but the little we know indicates that it went through the same upheavals that periodically wrack all the great states of today. Every now and then the parliament, or grand council, or steering committee or whatever the governing body was called suffered a wholesale purging, and as the old gang took to the hills a new gang came in. We know nothing of the issues involved, or of the personalities participating, but it is not unreasonable to assume that what happened then was substantially what happens now. Let us not be deceived by recalling that in Carthage, so far as the meagre record shows, the proletariat had no voice in the government, and that demagogy in our sense was thus impossible. Let us recall, rather, that demagogues do not operate on the proletariat only, but also on aristocracies, plutocracies and even kings and emperors. Nay, I have seen them, with my own eyes, operating upon bishops, university presidents and newspaper editors. They are the most adept practical psychologists of the race, and when they rise to their full gifts it is impossible to prevail against them by any means whatsoever, save only by the sorry means of setting another and worse gang of demagogues upon them.

Thus Carthage lived and had its being for 668 glorious years, constantly reaching out for new trade, setting up new bridgeheads on ever remoter and remoter coasts, and piling up wealth as no other nation had ever piled it up before. Its liners and tramp freighters went everywhere, and its ships of war controlled all the seas. Now and then, to be sure, some other nation objected to this relentless penetration, and especially to the monopoly that usually followed it, and there were bloody wars, but the Carthaginians took such unpleasantnesses in their stride, for they were well aware that blood was the price of admiralty. One of their wars lasted a hundred years, but they drew profits out of it all the while it was going on, and came out of it richer than ever. Every savage tribe from the Congo to the Baltic got a taste of their steel, and they did not hesitate to tackle the greatest empires. Even mighty Rome, at the apex of its power, found them formidable antagonists, and on several occasions they came within an ace of sacking the Imperial City itself. Altogether, it took the Romans 119 years to knock them off, and when it was accomplished at last it was made possible only by the fact that the blackamoors of Africa, tired at last of Carthaginian rule, joined Rome against them. As I looked out over the scene of what must have been the decisive battle of the war, I could not help wondering what these blackamoors had got out of the victory. Perhaps the Romans let them carry off a few women, and maybe a share of the lesser bric-a-brac. Otherwise, they got nothing, for the Romans grabbed everything really valuable for themselves, and a little while later they were running the blackamoors precisely as prisoners are run in an efficient house of correction, which is to say, precisely as the Carthaginians had been running them before the war.

The descendants of those poor people were before me as I pondered — laboriously plodding the Tunisian plain behind their archaic plows and spavined donkeys and camels, each surrounded by his ball of dust. It seemed a bleak and miserable life that they were leading, but I couldn't help adding to myself that they had at least survived. Of their old masters, the Carthaginians, there was nothing left save a Valhalla of blurred and incredible ghosts. I tried, though cold sober, to conjure up some of them as I contemplated their jumping-off place, but it was a vain undertaking, for even conjuring needs materials, and I had next to none. Who was the chief poet of Carthage in, say, the year 500 B.C., and what sort of poetry did he write? I asked myself the question, but that is as far as I got, for I was not too sure that Carthage had any poets, and if they existed no specimens of their work have come down to us. Well, then, what of the executive secretary of the Carthage Chamber of Commerce in the year 400? Here I got a little further, for a people as excessively commercial as the Carthaginians must have had a chamber of commerce, and it is impossible to imagine one without an executive secretary. I therefore imagined him, but having gone so far I was stalled again, for I could not figure out what he must have looked like, or what sort of office he did his work in, or how much of his time he devoted to port statistics and how much to writing speeches for the shipping magnates, grain exporters and bringers in of ivory, apes and peacocks who were his employers.

It was easier, somehow, to contrive plausible phantoms of lesser folk — for example, the stevedores down at the docks, the rowers of galleys, the cops patrolling their beats, the wine-sellers behind their bars, the hawkers of charms and images, the farmers in from the country with their loads of turnips and cabbages, the soldiers sparking the housemaids, the barbers with their sharp razors and clattering tongues. But even the barbers, when I got to them, hauled me up, for I was not sure that the Carthaginians shaved. Did the other Semites of that era? The portraits of Moses, Abraham and company in the art galleries of the world seem to indicate that they didn't, and I recalled that even the orthodox Jews of New York, up to the time they moved to the Bronx, still wore their beards. In the end the old gentry of Carthage gave me less trouble than any of the other folks, for the gentry are much the same everywhere. As the motorman of the Tunis trolley began to bang his gong and the bishop and I climbed aboard his car I was thinking of the ancient families that saw at one stroke the ruin of their nation and the annihilation of their own lines. Some of them, by 146 B.C., had been settled in Carthage for five or six hundred years, and their position in its society must have been quite the equal of that of the Percys in England. Whenever there was a public procession they marched at its head. No one ever dared to flout them, not even the politicoes in whose puppet-show they served as glittering dummies. They were the living symbols of half a millennium of Carthaginian power and glory, pomp and circumstance, and each of them was a living repository of honor, dignity, *noblesse oblige*. Not a few of them, I daresay, were so finely bred that they had lost the calves of their legs and were more or less hollow in the head, but they would not lie and they could not be bought. So they stood as the third Punic War came to its catastrophic end, and the ruffianly Romans closed in. By the time the burning and slaying, the raping and looting were over they had all vanished — and this is the first friendly mention that they have had in print, I suppose, for 2,088 years.

The bishop and I were silent as we were hauled back to Tunis, each sunk in his own thoughts. When the trolley-car finally stopped at the Tunis four corners we debarked from it and looked for a hack to haul us down to the wharf where a launch from our ship was waiting. At that moment a brisk and handsome young man, obviously an American, emerged from the assembled crowd, approached me politely, and asked me if I were not Mr. Mencken from Baltimore. When I replied that I was he introduced himself as a Baltimorean who had come out to the North African coast some years before, and was at present living in Tunis. I naturally asked him what he was doing there, and his reply was so astounding that I could only stare at him like an idiot. He was, he said, the manager of a baseball league stretching all along the coast, from Casablanca in the west to Cairo in the east, with a couple of outlying clubs in Syria and the Holy Land and another at Gibraltar. But where, I faltered, did he get his pitchers and catchers, his batters and fielders? What did the Moroccans, Berbers, Copts, Syrians, Arabs, Jews and the rest know about the national game of the United States?

His reply was that they knew a lot, for he had taught them. They were young fellows with plenty of enthusiasm in them, and hence quick to learn. Baseball, he said, was now the favorite sport along the whole south shore of the Mediterranean, and when two good teams met for an important game a large crowd turned out and there was a great deal of loud rooting. There was to be one the next day, and if I were free he would be delighted to have me see it as his guest. He had lived in Tunis so long, he said, that he was now almost a native, but his thoughts still turned to old Baltimore, and whenever he heard that a Baltimorean was in town he looked him up.

There was no time to cross-examine this amazing stranger, for the bishop and I had to get back to our ship, but he was a very well-appearing fellow, so I swallowed his tale without too much resistance. When I got back to Baltimore I found that it had been true in every detail. There was, in fact, a thick envelope of clippings about him in the morgue of the Baltimore *Sunpapers*. I went through those clippings with great interest, and was not surprised to discover that not one of them mentioned the fact that the home grounds of his Tunis club were on the site of what had once been Carthage.

XIX

PILGRIMAGE

[*1934*]

I WAS fifty-three years, five months and sixteen days old before ever I saw Jerusalem, and by that time, with Heaven itself beginning to loom menacingly on the skyline, my itch to sob at the holy places was naturally something less than frantic. I had not, in fact, gone to Palestine for the purpose of touring them, and had no intention of doing so; the only aim that I formulated to myself, in so far as I had any at all, was to visit and investigate the ruins of Gomorrah, the Hollywood of antiquity and the only rival of Sodom in the long and brilliant chronicles of sin. What attracted me to it, of course, was simply this almost unparalleled reputation for wickedness, for my experience of mankind had taught me that ill fame was commonly very much exaggerated, just as good fame was exaggerated. Hadn't I been to Hollywood itself, and found it to be almost if not quite as respectable as Newport

News, Va., or Natchez-under-the-Hill? What if I should discover evidence, on turning over the débris of Gomorrah, that it had been maligned by history, and even by Divine Revelation? In all this, I confess, there was a certain amount of attitudinizing, but I do not apologize for it, for it was attitudinizing more than anything else that led Columbus to discover America, as you will learn by reading Dr. Samuel E. Morison's excellent work, "Admiral of the Ocean Sea." In any case, I was willing to pay my own way, which was a good deal more than could be said for Columbus. If it cost me $250 to establish my thesis I'd be glad to meet the bills out of my own pocket and call it a day, and even if it ran to $500 or $1,000 I'd not be importuning the Queen of Spain for assistance or otherwise passing the hat.

Unhappily, I quickly learned, on inquiry in Jerusalem, that the brimstone and fire described in Genesis xix, 24 had been so effective that nothing remained of Gomorrah save a name to scare Sunday-schools. Even on the elementary question of its site all the local authorities seemed to be at odds. One of Cook's agents, a young Welshman speaking five languages, told me that it was somewhere in a swamp south of the Dead Sea, and offered to get me there in a Buick, with a chauffeur, an interpreter and three meals a day included, at a flat rate of $18.75 *per diem;* but while I was negotiating with him a Syrian employed by the Palestine Exploration Fund, and speaking seven languages, horned in with a noisy declaration that the true location was fifty miles away, on the *north* shore of the sea. Leaving these experts snorting at each other, I returned to the King David Hotel outside the walls and there consulted the *portier*, an intelligent Swiss speaking nine languages. He told me that what remained of the town was really in the bed of the sea, and offered in proof the fact that the workmen of the English company engaged in dredging the bottom for potash often brought up bones, musical instruments and bogus jewelry. This shook me, and I devoted the next morning to looking into the matter more particularly. Before noon I had accumulated six more opinions, all of them positive and authoritative, but each differing from the rest. By that time I was in a considerable sweat, for it is warmish in Jerusalem even in Winter, so I finally adopted the escapist theory that Jahveh had made a really all-out job of Gomorrah, as the Romans had of Carthage, and abandoned my plan to explore its ruins.

My decision left me with some unexpected leisure on my hands, and I employed it in moseying about Jerusalem, the glory of Israel as Ireland is of God. It turned out to be a town of about the size of Savannah, Ga., or South Bend, Ind., but differing radically from both. There had been, a short while before, some gang fights between Jews and Arabs, and they were destined, a little while later, to fall upon one another in the grand manner, but at the time of my visit, which was in 1934, there was a hiatus in these hostilities and I was not molested, though I was warned by an English cop that some sassy Arab might have at me with a camel flop as an infidel or some super-orthodox Jew might hoot me as a *chazirfresser*. Most of the so-called streets I traversed were not more than ten feet wide and a good many of them ended in dead walls. Nearly all were lined with so-called *suks*, or bazaars — a series of holes in the wall not much larger than kitchenettes. In each *suk* lurked a merchant sitting cross-legged, and in front of each merchant were spread his wares — most often, only sleazy looking rugs, tarnished brass vessels full of dents, crude pottery of the thunder-mug species, and other such gimcrackery. Having just come from Cairo, where some of the *suks* approximate the glitter of Fifth avenue specialty shops, and Algiers, where many of them offer wines and liquors and there is a bawdy-house every block or so, I was not impressed by those of Jerusalem.

There was a good deal of crowding and jostling in the streets, but what made walking really unpleasant was the paving. It was kept in reasonable repair, but it consisted predominantly of cobbles, and they were made of a soft native limestone that became as smooth as glass under foot traffic, and quite as slippery. Having come down a couple of times, I paused in a little plaza to take stock of my injuries, and there saw a British soldier in full equipment land on his *tochos* with a fearful clatter. When I helped him to his feet he told me that he had served in H. M. Army for twelve years, in posts ranging from Gibraltar to Ceylon and including such hells as Aden and Rangoon, but that Jerusalem, in his judgment, was the bloodiest goddam place of them all. It was a lucky day, he said, when the cobbles fetched him less than five times, and there were bad days when he got back to barracks with his caboose as badly macerated as a pug's nose and ears. He spoke in favorable terms of the destruction of the city by the Romans in the year 70 A.D., though he apparently thought that the date of the job was as recent as Napoleonic times. A man of speculative mind, he tried to figure out how long it would take a smart battery of artillery posted on the Mount of Olives to knock the whole bloody settlement to pieces, and his guess was that it could be bloody well done in half an hour. He was, he said, bloody hot for trying it, and he hoped that it would be done in some bloody future war.

This soldier told me, somewhat to my surprise, that I was standing directly in front of the Church of the Holy Sepulchre, and advised me with a derisive wink to have a look at the interior. A few weeks before, he said, the walls had cracked and the building threatened to tumble in, but since then it had been shored up by the British authorities and was now reasonably safe. Entering by a small door at a cost of an American quarter, collected by an Armenian clergyman in long whiskers, I found myself in what appeared, at first glance, to be the midway of a small carnival. The whole roof was hung with shabby banners and streamers, and pendent from them were almost innumerable lamps and lanterns, some lighted and smoking but the majority out of service. The floor was divided by low railings into four or five sections, and I learned from a sort of map that had been handed to me at the door that each belonged to one or another branch of the Christian Church — the Roman, the Greek Orthodox, the Armenian, the Nestorian, and so on. Each section was manned by ecclesiastics of the branch in charge of it. The actual Sepulchre, it appeared, was in charge of the Copts — whether by a permanent arrangement or by some sort of rotation I was not informed. It cost me another quarter to see it, and the priest in charge threw a good deal of hocus-pocus into showing it. What he finally had to offer, after cautioning me in half a dozen languages to keep my hat off, was simply a hole probably ten feet wide, twenty feet long and twelve feet deep, hollowed out of the solid rock and reached by a stone stairway. Obviously enough, at least to anyone familiar with John xix, 41, as I was, it was bogus; indeed it was bogus by the Synoptic Gospels also, for unless Joseph of Arimathea was a reincarnation of Samson no one could imagine him rolling a stone large enough to close it. But I kept my doubts to myself, bowed politely to the rev. Copt, and shoved off to see what the Jews and Moslems had to offer, for Jerusalem is a holy city to both of them just as it is to Christians.

The Moslems, I found, put on nothing describable as a first-rate attraction, and in fact discouraged visits to their sacred stands by unbelievers, and the best Jewish show currently playing was that at the famous Wailing Wall. A British cop showing me a short cut by way of the old city ramparts, I found the place without any difficulty. It was a huge excavation in the rock recalling those that laborious Italians used to make in the Archean underpinnings of Manhattan island in the days when men of vision were still building sky-scrapers. It was lined with masonry, and one of the walls was considerably higher than the others. At the bottom of this high wall was the wailing place, and as I came down the long stairway to the bottom of the great pit perhaps twenty-five Jews were lined up, all of them with their faces to the wall. I naturally expected to hear some hubbub, but save for an occasional mild shriek or groan the wailing was carried on *pianissimo*, and one had to come close to a given Jew to hear him at all. Their operations were apparently ritualistic in character, for each had a book in front of him, held up against the wall, and some of them followed the text with their forefingers. At one end of the pit stood a camp-stool and a little camp-table, and on the stool sat a British sergeant in his shirt-sleeves, intent upon a copy of the *News of the World* spread out upon the table. I assumed that he was there to protect the Jews against the Arabs, who might have bombarded them very easily from the tops of the walls, but when I tackled him he said not.

"I have my men up there," he explained, "and they keep all suspicious characters moving. Before an Arab could let go with a dead cat they would have nippers on him, and he would be on his way to three months hard. What I am down in this bloody hole for is to keep the peace among the Jews. They are all very religious fellows, and so they tend to hate each other. Suppose a Jew from Baghdad comes down in the morning and finds that the place he used yesterday has been grabbed by a Jew from Salonika. Does he say, 'Excuse me, Mister, but you have my pitch. Would you mind shoving over a bit?' Not at all. In the first place, the Baghdad lingo is as different from Salonikan as English is from French, and both speak Hebrew with thick accents, the one, let us say, like an Irishman and the other like a Welshman. So they simply screech at each other, and in two minutes, if I didn't jump into the ring and make them break, they would be pulling whiskers, and then their friends would join in, and we'd have a couple of jobs for the ambulance. But it's not hard to handle them if you know how. All I have to do is to let go with my fists, and it is all over. I have been sitting here for six months, and I know most of the steady customers. Some of them, I hear, have been at it off and on for years. It is a kind of trade with them. Nine out of ten are as peaceable as so many blind men. When a shindy is going on at one end of the wall the old fellows at the other end keep on wailing. I have been told that it has been going on since Adam's time. What they are wailing about I don't know, though I have heard two or three different stories. You can never believe anything you hear in Jerusalem. The place is full of liars."

Slipping the instructive sergeant a five-cent American cigar and wishing him many happy returns of the day, I went back to the King David Hotel, and there hired a car to take me to Bethlehem, five miles out of town. The driver, a Soudanese Negro who had been a dragoman in Cairo and spoke very fair English, pointed out the places of interest along the road. The only one that I remember was the Y.M.C.A., a huge structure not far from the King David, resembling in a way a country-club in Florida and in another way the General Motors building at a world's fair. I asked the driver how so large an establishment could be supported in Jerusalem, for Protestants are almost as rare there as in South Boston or the Bronx. He replied that the money came from America, and that the actual patrons were Moslems and Jews. The Moslems, he said, went in for track work in the gymnasium, and the Jews patronized the free classes in double-entry bookkeeping, foreign exchange and scientific salesmanship. On the common ground of their dislike of Christians they met amicably, and there had never been any rough stuff at the Y, even when riots were going on at its very door. I ventured to suggest that maybe this was due to the calming influence of the Y.M.C.A. secretaries, and asked the Soudanese if they had converted any of the Moslems or Jews to their Rotarian theology. His only reply was to laugh. He said that the Salvation Army, a much more powerful theological engine than the Y.M.C.A., had been banging away in Jerusalem for years, but that its only converts to date were a few soldiers drummed out of the British Army, a few drink-crazed Scandinavian sailors wandering in from Haifa and Jaffa, and a meagre haul of other such poor fish. It was just as unlikely for a Moslem to turn Methodist, he said, as it would be for a Methodist to turn Moslem. Protestantism had no more chance in Palestine, he went on, than cannibalism would have in England. Not only were the Moslems and Jews unanimously against it; the Latin, Greek, Abyssinian, Armenian, Coptic and other old-fashioned dirt Christians were even more against it, and spent a great deal of time talking against it. The Holy Land, he said, did not have any taste for novelty, and was generally hostile to strangers. Nearly everything in sight was at least ten thousand years old, and the people distrusted anything newer. The great majority of them, including most of the Jews who were there before Zionism got afoot, preferred Turkish rule to that of the English, who were constantly shoring up tumbledown churches and mosques, arresting poor folk for clubbing donkeys or committing nuisances up alleys, issuing insane regulations for the disposal of garbage, and otherwise making pests of themselves. The Turks believed in living and letting live, and were thus esteemed. To be sure, they had laid on heavy taxes, but it was always possible to get out of paying more than a small part by seeing the right persons, and no tax they ever laid on was as heavy as those laid on by the incorruptible English.

The Soudanese told me that the only thing worth seeing at Bethlehem was the Church of the Nativity — for the rest, he said, the town consisted only of souvenir shoppes full of relics made in Japan —, so I proceeded to take a look at the sacred edifice as soon as we got to the town. It was managed jointly, the Soudanese explained, by monks of the Armenian, Greek and Latin rites, and not infrequently they got into lamentable disputes over nuances of dogma, and had been known, historically, to back up revelation with a certain amount of eye-gouging, nose-biting and whiskers-yanking. I was amazed to discover, when I got to the place, that its builders back in the Ages of Faith had apparently forgotten to give it a front door, just as Thomas Jefferson, centuries later, was to forget to provide a stairway in his mansion at Monticello. The entrance, in fact, was a mere hole in the wall, and in order to get through it I had to bend almost double. Arriving inside, I was even more amazed to discover that there was a large and even huge door in the rear wall — one big enough, in fact, to let in a Fifth avenue bus. Why wasn't it used instead of the hole in front? I asked the question of everyone I encountered in Bethlehem who could speak English, but never got a satisfactory answer. On my return to Jerusalem I renewed my inquiries, and was told by the Swiss *portier* at the King David that the hole was used simply because the monks believed that putting customers to a little discomfort threw them into a mortified frame of mind, and so promoted their fear of God and made them generous with contributions. They had read in some quackish forerunner of "How to Make Friends and Influence People" that it was sound psychology to make the pious sweat a bit, lest pride consume them. If that was actually their theory, then it certainly failed to work in my own case, for I emerged from the hole in the front wall, after a scant fifteen minutes inside, full of wayward doubts and cholers. I even began to suspect that the whole establishment was a fake, just as the Church of the Holy Sepulchre was a fake. How, indeed, could any rational person reconcile the elaborate marble grotto that the monks had shown me with the manger described in Luke ii, 7, 12 and 16?

Back in Jerusalem, I took a walk that evening to work off my dubieties, and, on encountering a sort of information bureau run by the Jewish Agency, dropped in to pick up some of its literature. One of the young Jews in attendance asked me to sign the visitors' book and I did so. By the time I got back to the hotel a couple of smart agents of the Agency, both speaking fluent English, were waiting for me. It appeared that they had recognized my name as that of a man connected with the press, and had dropped in to say that if I cared to make a tour of the Jewish colonies to the north of Jerusalem they were at my service. This friendly invitation sounded so attractive that I accepted at once. As a result, one of the agents and I started out in a car very early the next morning, and by nightfall had accomplished one of the most charming trips I have ever made in this life. The day was fine, the roads were good, the car was fast, and the agent who steered me, Mr. A. L. Fellman, was an intelligent young man speaking English, Yiddish, Arabic and Hebrew, with family connections in my native Baltimore. Nearly everything worth seeing in Palestine, he told me, was north of Jerusalem, and we covered virtually all of it in the one day, for the distance from Jerusalem to the line of the Sea of Galilee, Nazareth and

Mount Carmel is less than seventy-five miles. The road northward runs almost straight, but we debouched from it often, and at the end of the day our speedometer showed a run of 350 kilometers. At one time we ran along the Jordan for a dozen or more miles and made a foray across it into Trans-Jordan, which looked a good deal like the worst parts of Arizona. Stopping at noon for a hearty *kosher* lunch at Tiberias, on the Sea of Galilee — I recall that there were two soups, three kinds of meat, and four kinds of pastry —, we struck westward over the Galilean highlands, and after seeing the place where the Gadarene swine were possessed by devils and leaped into the water, the birthplace of Mary Magdalene, the scene of the miracle at Cana — often mentioned favorably in the American newspapers of the days of Prohibition —, the town of Nazareth, and the ancient battlefield of Armageddon, we landed finally at Haifa on the sea coast. On the long way we stopped at half a dozen of the Jewish colonies, and had friendly palavers with their public relations agents, most of whom, I found, could speak either English or German, and often both.

These colonies interested me greatly, if only because of the startling contrast they presented to the adjacent Arab farms. The Arabs of the Holy Land, like those of the other Mediterranean countries, are probably the dirtiest, orneriest and most shiftless people who regularly make the first pages of the world's press. To find a match for them one must resort to the oakies now translated from Oklahoma to suffering California, or to the half-simian hill-billies of the Appalachian chain. Though they have been in contact with civilization for centuries, and are credited by many fantoddish professors with having introduced it into Europe, they still plow their miserable fields with the tool of Abraham, to wit, a bent stick. In the morning, as Fellman and I spun up the highroad to the north, I saw them going to work, each with his preposterous plow over his back, and in the evening, as we went westward across Galilee, I saw them returning home in the same way. Their draft animals consisted of anything and everything — a milch cow, a camel, a donkey, a wife, a stallion, a boy, an ox, a mule, or some combination thereof. Never, even in northwestern Arkansas or the high valleys of Tennessee, have I seen more abject and anemic farms. Nine-tenths of them were too poor even to grow weeds: they were simply reverting to the gray dust into which the land of Moab to the eastward has long since fallen. As for the towns in which the Arabs lived, they resembled nothing so much as cemeteries in an advanced state of ruin. The houses were built of fieldstone laid without mortar, and all the roofs were lopsided and full of holes. From these forlorn hovels ragged women peeped at us from behind their greasy veils, and naked children popped out to steal a scared look and then pop back. Of edible fauna there was scarcely a trace. Now and then I saw a sad cow, transiently reprieved from the plow, and in one village there was a small flock of chickens, but the cows always seemed to be dying of pellagra or beri-beri, and the chickens were small, skinny and mangy.

These Arab villages were scattered all about, but most of them were on hilltops, as if the sites had been chosen for defense. Sweeping down from them into the valleys below were the lands of the immigrant Jews. The contrast was so striking as to be almost melodramatic. It was as if a series of Ozark corn-patches had been lifted out of their native wallows and set down amidst the lush plantations of the Pennsylvania Dutch. On one side of a staggering stone hedge were the bleak, miserable fields of the Arabs, and on the other side were the almost tropical demesnes of the Jews, with long straight rows of green field crops, neat orchards of oranges, lemons and pomegranates, and frequent wood-lots of young but flourishing eucalyptus. Fat cows grazed in the meadows, there were herds of goats eating weeds, and every barnyard swarmed with white Leghorn chickens. In place of the bent sticks of the Arabs, the Jews operated gang-plows drawn by tractors, and nearly every colony had a machine-shop, a saw-mill and a cannery. The contrast between the buildings on the two sides of the hedges was as remarkable as that between the fields. The Arabs, as I have said, lived in squalid huts letting in wind, rain and flying things, and their barns were hardly more than corrals, but the Jews lived in glistening new stucco houses recalling the more delirious suburbs of Los Angeles, and their animals were housed quite as elegantly as themselves. The architecture on display, I should add, caused me to cough sadly behind my hand, but it had at least some relevance to history and the terrain, for the general effect was genuinely oriental, as indeed it is in Los Angeles. The Jews appeared to be very proud of their habitations, for every time Fellman and I stopped at one and found the householder at home he insisted on showing us through it, and almost always pointed with swelling emotion to its tiled floors, its screened doors and its running water in the kitchen.

These Jews, however, appeared to spend but a small part of their time admiring their quarters: virtually all their waking hours were given to hard labor in the fields. In the larger colonies they did not even come in for meals, but were fed from a lunch-wagon working out of the central kitchen. Nor were their wives idle, for cooking was their job, and in addition they usually had to attend to the chickens and milk the cows. In some of the more advanced-thinking colonies the care of their children was taken from them to give them more time for these chores, and handed over to professionals, always including a trained nurse with a sharp eye for loose teeth and wormy tonsils. A mother, of course, could see her offspring in the intervals of her labors, but until they were six or seven years old they slept in dormitories attached to the schools, and she was not responsible for either their alimentation or their indoctrination. Fellman and I dropped in at several schools, and inspected the young inmates. They looked as healthy and happy as the prize babies whose pictures appear in the rotogravure advertisements of the milk companies.

It was pleasant roving about these luxuriant farms and palavering with the laborious and earnest men and women who ran them, but it didn't take long to discover that their passion for a constructive idealism was accompanied by the usual and apparently inevitable aches and pains. Much of the land they wrestled with was fertile enough, once the poisonous Arabs had been cleared off it, but there were other tracts that had suffered so badly by the misuse of centuries that getting them back to fecundity was an appallingly onerous business. They not only needed draining and grading and the repair of washouts; they also needed a long course of nursing, with heavy expenditures for fertilizers. Would this coddling ever really pay? Would the soil thus restored ever provide sufficient livings for the heavy work forces needed to restore it? On that point I found a certain amount of doubt, concealed only defectively by tall talk. So long as there was a steady flow of money from Zionists all over the earth the problem would not be pressing, but what if that flow were ever cut off? Also, what would happen if another world war interrupted overseas trade, and left Palestine to butter its own parsnips? One of the chief customers for the excellent oranges of the country, in 1934, was Germany. Could the Jews, with such markets closed, live on vitamins alone? I suspect that many a sweating colonist, his back bent in the field, occasionally let his mind play upon such unhappy questions, and if not in the field then in his scant hours of ease of an evening, with his radio blaring music from Berlin, Vienna and Rome, and an occasional whiff of jazz from points west.

But this fear of remote and still theoretical catastrophe was much less apparent than a fear of closer and even more unpleasant possibilities. The Arabs, who had been dispossessed of some of their best (as well as of some of their worst) lands, still hung about, and there was little reassurance in their dark and envious eyes. They blamed the *effendi* landlords in Cairo and Damascus for selling them out to the Jews, but they blamed the Jews even more for trading with the *effendis*, if only because the Jews were directly under their noses. It had been assumed by the pumpers up of Zionist enthusiasm, and in fact announced confidently, that the example of the colonists would lift these degraded step-brothers out of their ancient shiftlessness and imbecility, and make competent and successful farmers of them, but the event had proved that they were as incapable of competent farming as so many Florida crackers. Some of them had tried more or less earnestly, but all save an infinitesimal minority had failed. In plain view of the broad and smiling fields of the smart and diligent Jews they were still plowing idiotically with their bent sticks, and if Allah, by any chance, sent them more than eight bushels of wheat to an acre they hustled off to Mecca to give thanks. Like all such Chandala they ascribed their congenital unfitness to the villainy of their betters, and not infrequently they tried to cure it in the ancient Chandala manner. That is to say, they took to assassination. Already in 1934 it was becoming common for a Jew at work on the slopes making down to the Jordan to be knocked off by a shot from the other side of the river. The British had built concrete blockhouses all through that lovely country and armed them with machine-guns, but those machine-guns offered no protection to Jews on outlying farms, and by the time a squad of soldiers got to the scene of a murder the Arab was lost in the wilds of Trans-Jordan. Nor could the poor Jews do anything effective in defense of themselves. I saw a number of them plowing with rifles strapped to their backs, but it was usually in the back that the brave Arabs shot them, and when that happened the rifle went down with the man. Altogether, there was an air of dread hanging over the border, and I was glad when we struck into the Galilean high country. As we mounted the first hill we looked back at the Sea of Galilee and saw a rainbow set prettily upon it, but if that rainbow was actually a promise, as recollections of Genesis IX, 16 suggested, then it was only too obviously a false one. Only a few years later the whole land was running with blood, and then came the even greater calamity of World War II. I wonder as I write what has been the fate of some of the hopeful and persevering Jews I met on that beautiful Winter day. Most of them, I trust, are still alive, but I am not too sure that those who are still alive are more fortunate than those who are dead.

Perhaps appropriately, I made my exit from the Holy Land by way of the battlefield of Armageddon, which began to soak up gore in the remotest mists of the past, and had seen its last battle so recently as 1918, when Allenby and the Turks rounded out their little war by fighting all over it. No military geographer was needed to explain its immemorial popularity among professional bloodletters. The great barrier of the Syrian mountains here ends in the promontory of Mount Carmel, and the only way for an army to move northward or southward in any comfort is by way of the narrow beach which separates Mount Carmel from the sea. By that route all the hordes of antiquity had moved or tried to move. Here the Hittites met the Egyptians, the Egyptians met the Persians, the Persians met the Greeks, and the Jews were slaughtered by one and all. Below the narrow pass the land widens out into a wide and almost flat plain, and it was on it that the ancient battles joined. There is probably no more likely battlefield on earth; it seems to have been made for the marching and counter-marching of infantry, and dashing cavalry charges. As we rolled over it I could not help thinking of the hundreds of thousands of miserable John Does who had watered it, over so many ages, with their blood. More than one long forgotten captain won his bays there, and more than one great empire came crashing down. If it were in America it would be dotted with hideous monuments to the Fifth Pennsylvania and the Tenth Wisconsin, and there would be guides to carry tourists over it, and plenty of hot-dog and Coca-Cola stands to stoke them. But at Armageddon I couldn't find so much as a marker or a flag. Over the dust of the immemorial and innumerable dead some Jewish colonists were driving Ford tractors hitched to plows. It was much safer there than along the Jordan shore, and so they looked contented and even somewhat complacent. But I noticed that the earth their plowshares were turning up was redder than the red hills of Georgia. In the afternoon sunshine, in fact, it was precisely the color of blood.

XX

BEATERS OF BREASTS

[*1936*]

On September 1, in the presidential campaign year of 1936, I received an office chit from Paul Patterson, publisher of the Baltimore *Sunpapers*, proposing that I go to Boston to cover the Harvard tercentenary orgies, then just getting under way. On September 3, after a day given over, at least in theory, to prayer and soul-searching, I replied as follows:

> The more I think over the Harvard project, the less it lifts me. I'd much prefer to join Alf Landon. I like politicoes much better than I like professors. They sweat more freely and are more amusing.

My prayer and soul-searching, of course, were purely bogus, as such exercises only too often are. I had actually made up my mind in favor of the politicians a great many years before, to wit, in

1900 or thereabout, when I was still an infant at the breast in journalism. They shocked me a little at my first intimate contact with them, for I had never suspected, up to then, that frauds so bold and shameless could flourish in a society presumably Christian, and under the eye of a putatively watchful God. But as I came to know them better and better I began to develop a growing admiration, if not for their virtue, then at least for their professional virtuosity, and at the same time I discovered that many of them, in their private character, were delightful fellows, whatever their infamies *ex officio*. This appreciation of them, in the years following, gradually extended itself into a friendly interest in quacks of all sorts, whether theological, economic, military, philanthropic, judicial, literary, musical or sexual, and including even the professorial, and in the end that interest made me a sort of expert on the science of rooking the confiding, with a large acquaintance among practitioners of every species. But though I thus threw a wide net I never hauled in any fish who seemed to me to be the peers of the quacks political — not, indeed, by many a glittering inch. Even the Freudians when they dawned, and the chiropractors, and the penologists, and the social engineers, and the pedagogical wizards of Teachers College, Columbia, fell a good deal short of many Congressmen and Senators that I knew, not to mention Governors of sovereign American states. The Governors, in fact, were for long my favorites, for they constituted a class of extraordinarily protean rascals, and I remember a year when, of the forty-eight then in office, four were under indictment by grand juries, and one was actually in jail. Of the rest, seven were active Ku Kluxers, three were unreformed labor leaders, two were dipsomaniacs, five were bogus war heroes, and another was an astrologer.

My high opinion of political mountebanks remains unchanged to this day, and I suspect that when the history of our era is written at last it may turn out that they have been one of America's richest gifts to humanity. On only one point do I discover any doubt, and that is on the point whether those who really believe in their hocus-pocus — for example, Woodrow Wilson — are to be put higher or lower, in entertainment value, to those who are too smart — for example, Huey Long. Perhaps the question answers itself, for very few of the second class, in the long run, are able to resist their own buncombe, and I daresay that Huey, if the Japs had not cut him down prematurely, would have ended by believing more or less in his share-the-wealth apocalypse, though not, of course, to the extent of sharing his share. After the death of William Jennings Bryan, in 1926, I printed an estimate of his life and public services which dismissed him as a quack pure and unadulterated, but in the years since I have come to wonder if that was really just. When, under the prodding of Clarence Darrow, he made his immortal declaration that man is not a mammal, it seemed to me to be a mere bravura piece by a quack sure that his customers would take anything. But I am now more than half convinced that Jennings really believed it, just as he believed that Jonah swallowed the whale. The same phenomenon is often visible in other fields of quackery, especially the theological. More than once I have seen a Baptist evangelist scare himself by his own alarming of sinners, and quite as often I have met social workers who actually swallowed at least a third of their sure-cures for all the sorrows of the world. Let us not forget that Lydia Pinkham, on her deathbed, chased out her doctors and sent for a carboy of her Vegetable Compound, and that Karl Marx (though not Engels) converted himself to Socialism in his declining years.

It amazes me that no one has ever undertaken a full-length psychological study of Bryan, in the manner of Gamaliel Bradford and Lytton Strachey, for his life was long and full of wonders. My own contacts with him, unhappily, were rather scanty, though I reported his performances, off and on, from 1904 to 1926, a period of nearly a quarter of a century. The first time I saw him show in the grand manner was at the Democratic national convention of 1904, in St. Louis. He had been the party candidate for the presidency in 1896 and 1900, and was to be the candidate again in 1908, but in 1904 the gold Democrats were on top and he was rejected in favor of Alton B. Parker, a neat and clean but bewildered judge from somewhere up the Hudson, now forgotten by all save political antiquarians. Jennings made a stupendous fight against Parker, and was beaten in the end only by a resort to gouging *a posteriori* and kneeing below the belt. On a hot, humid night, with the hall packed, he elbowed his way to the platform to deliver what he and everyone else thought would be his valedictory. He had prepared for it by announcing that he had come down with laryngitis and could scarcely speak, and as he began his speech it was in a ghostly whisper. That was long before the day of loud-speakers, so the gallery could not hear him, and in a minute it was howling to him to speak louder, and he was going through the motion of trying to do so. In his frayed alpaca coat and baggy pants he was a pathetic figure, and that, precisely, is what he wanted to appear.

But galleries are always brutal, and this one was worse than most. It kept on howling, and in a little while the proceedings had to be suspended while the sergeants-at-arms tried to restore order. How long the hiatus continued I forget, but I well remember how it ended. One of the dignitaries in attendance was the late J. Ham Lewis, then in the full splendor of his famous pink whiskers. He sat at a corner of the platform where everyone in the house could see him, and so sitting, with the fetid miasma from

15,000 Democrats rising about him, he presently became thirsty. Calling a page, he sent out for a couple of bottles of beer, and when they came in, sweating with cold, he removed the caps with a gold opener, parted his vibrissae with a lordly gesture, and proceeded to empty the beer down his esophagus. The galleries, forgetting poor Jennings, rose on their hind legs and gave Ham three loud cheers, and when they were over it was as if an electric spark had been discharged, for suddenly there was quiet, and Jennings could go on.

The uproar had nettled him, for he was a vain fellow, and when he uttered his first words it was plain that either his indignation had cured his laryngitis or he had forgotten it. His magnificent baritone voice rolled out clearly and sonorously, and in two minutes he had stilled the hostility of the crowd and was launched upon a piece of oratory of the very first chop. There were hundreds of politicians present who had heard his Cross of Gold speech in Chicago in 1896, and they were still more or less under its enchantment, but nine-tenths of them were saying the next day that this St. Louis speech was even more eloquent, even more gaudy, even more overpowering. Certainly I listened to it myself with my ears wide open, my eyes apop and my reportorial pencil palsied. It swept up on wave after wave of sound like the *finale* of the first movement of Beethoven's Eroica, and finally burst into such coruscations that the crowd first gasped and then screamed. "You *may* say," roared Jennings, "that I have not fought a good fight. [*A pause.*] You *may* say that I have not run a good race. [*A longer pause, with dead silence in the galleries.*] But *no* man [*crescendo*] shall say [*a catch in the baritone voice*] *that I have not kept the faith!!!!*"

That was long, long ago, in a hot and boozy town, in the decadent days of an American era that is now as far off as the Würm Glaciation, but I remember it as clearly as if it were last night. What a speech, my masters! What a speech! Like all really great art, it was fundamentally simple. The argument in it, so far as I can recall it at all, was feeble, and the paraphrase of II Timothy IV, 7 was obvious. But how apt, how fit and meet, how tremendously effective! If the galleries had been free to vote, Bryan would have been nominated on the spot, and to the tune of ear-splitting hallelujahs. Even as it was, there was an ominous stirring among the delegates, boughten though most of them were, and the leaders, for ten minutes, were in a state of mind not far from the panicky. I well recall how they darted through the hall, slapping down heresy here and encouraging the true faith there. Bryan, always the perfect stage manager, did not wait for this painful afterglow. He knew that he was done for, and he was too smart to be on hand for the formal immolation. Instead, he climbed down from the platform and made his slow way out of the hall, his huge catfish mouth set in a hard line, his great eyes glittering, his black hair clumped in sweaty locks over his epicycloid dome. He looked poor and shabby and battered, but he was pathetic no more. The Money Power had downed him, but his soul was marching on. Some one in the galleries started to sing " John Brown's Body " in a voice of brass, but the band leader shut it off hastily by breaking into " The Washington *Post* March." Under cover of the banal strains the leaders managed to restore law and order in the ranks. The next morning Parker was nominated, and on the Tuesday following the first Monday of the ensuing November he was laid away forever by Roosevelt I.

I missed Bryan's come-back in 1908, but I saw him often after that, and was present, as I have recorded, at his Gethsemane among the Bible searchers at Dayton, Tenn., though I had left town before he actually ascended into Heaven. He was largely responsible for the nomination of Woodrow Wilson at Baltimore in 1912, and was rewarded for his services by being made Secretary of State. In New York, in 1924, after howling against Wall Street for nearly three weeks, he accepted the nomination of its agent and attorney, John W. Davis, of Piping Rock, W. Va., and took in payment the nomination of his low comedy brother, Charlie, to second place on the ticket. During the great war upon the Rum Demon he hung back until the triumph of Prohibition began to seem inevitable, and then leaped aboard the band-wagon with loud, exultant gloats. In brief, a fraud. But I find myself convinced, nevertheless, that his support of the Good Book against Darwin and company was quite sincere — that is, as sincerity runs among politicoes. When age began to fetch him the fear of Hell burgeoned out of his unconscious, and he died a true Christian of the Hookworm Belt, full of a malignant rage against the infidel.

Bryan was essentially and incurably a yap, and never had much of a following in the big cities. At the New York convention of 1924 the Tammany galleries razzed him from end to end of his battle against the Interests, and then razzed him again, and even more cruelly, when he sold out for the honor of the family. He made speeches nearly every day, but they were heard only in part, for the moment he appeared on the platform the Al Smith firemen in the galleries began setting off their sirens and the cops on the floor began shouting orders and pushing people about. Thus the setting was not favorable for his oratory, and he made a sorry showing. But when he had a friendly audience he was magnificent. I heard all the famous rhetoricians of his generation, from Chauncey M. Depew to W. Bourke Cockran, and it is my sober judgment, standing on the brink of eternity, that he was the greatest of them all. His voice had something of the caressing richness of Julia Marlowe's, and he could think upon his feet much better than at a desk. The average impromptu speech, taken down by a stenographer, is found to be a bedlam of puerile clichés, thumping non sequiturs and limping, unfinished sentences. But Jennings emitted English that was clear, flowing and sometimes not a little elegant, in the best sense of the word. Every sentence had a beginning, a middle and an end. The argument, three times out of four, was idiotic, but it at least hung together.

I never traveled with him on his tours of the cow country, but it was my good fortune to accompany various other would-be heirs to Washington and Lincoln on theirs, and I always enjoyed the experience, though it meant heavy work for a reporter, and a certain amount of hardship. No politician can ever resist a chance to make a speech, and sometimes, in the regions where oratory is still esteemed, that chance offers twenty or thirty times a day. What he has to say is seldom worth hearing, but he roars it as if it were gospel, and in the process of wearing out his vocal chords he also wears out the reporters. More than once, accompanying such a geyser, I have been hard at it for eighteen hours out of the twenty-four, and have got nothing properly describable as a meal until 11.30 p.m. Meanwhile, unless there is an occasional lay-over in some hotel, it is hard to keep clean, and in consequence after a couple of weeks of campaigning the entourage of a candidate for the highest secular office under God begins to smell like a strike meeting of longshoremen.

Of all the hopefuls I have thus accompanied on their missionary journeys — it is perhaps only a coincidence that each and every one of them was licked — the most amusing was Al Smith. By the time he made his campaign in 1928 he was very well known to the country, and so he attracted large crowds everywhere. Sometimes, of course, those crowds were a good deal more curious than cordial, for Al passed, in the pellagra and chigger latitudes, as no more than a secret agent of the Pope, and it was generally believed that he had machine-guns aboard his campaign train, and was ready to turn them loose at a word from Rome. But the only time he met with actual hostility was not in the tall grass but in the metropolis of Louisville, and the persons who tried to fetch him there were not credulous yokels but city slickers. His meeting was held in a large hall, and every inch of it was jammed. When Al and his party got to the place they found it uncomfortably warm, but that was hardly surprising, for big crowds always engender calories. But by the time the candidate rose to speak the heat was really extraordinary, and before he was half way through his speech he was sweating so copiously that he seemed half drowned. The dignitaries on the platform sweated too, and so did the vulgar on the floor and in the galleries. Minute by minute the temperature seemed to increase, until finally it became almost unbearable. When Al shut down at last, with his collar a rag and his shirt and pants sticking to his hide, the thermometer must have stood at 100 degrees at least, and there were plenty who guessed that it stood at 110. Not until the campaign party got back to its train did the truth reach it. There then appeared an apologetic committee with the news that the city administration of Louisville, which was currently Republican, had had its goons fire up the boilers under the hall, deliberately and with malice prepense. The plan had been to wreck the meeting by frying it, but the plotters had underestimated the endurance of a politico with an audience in front of him, and also the endurance of an American crowd feasting its eyes upon a celebrated character. It took Al twenty-four hours to cool off, but I had noted no falling off in his oratorical amperage. He had, in fact, hollered even louder than usual, and his steaming customers had howled with delight. What his speech was about I can't tell you, and neither, I daresay, could anyone else who was present.

The truth is that some of his most effective harangues in that campaign were probably more or less unintelligible to himself. The common report was that he knew nothing about national issues, and that he had never, in fact, been across the North river before he was nominated, or even so much as looked across, so he carried a Brain Trust with him to help him prove that this report was all a lie, and its members prepared the first draft of every one of his set speeches. Its chief wizard was the famous Mrs. Belle Israels Moskowitz, but she did not travel with the candidate; instead, she remained at his G.H.Q. in New York, bossing a huge staff of experts in all the known departments of human knowledge, and leaving the field work to two trusties — the Hon. Joseph M. Proskauer, a justice of the Supreme Court of New York, and the Hon. Bernard L. Shientag, then a justice of the New York City court. The two learned judges and their secretaries sweated almost as hard every day as Al sweated in that hall in Louisville. They had a car to themselves, and it was filled with files, card indexes and miscellaneous memoranda supplied from time to time by Mrs. Moskowitz. Every morning they would turn out bright and early to concoct Al's evening speech — usually on some such unhappy and unfathomable subject (at least to the candidate himself) as the tariff, the League of Nations, Farm Relief, the Alaskan fisheries, or the crimes of the Chicago Board of Trade. They would work away at this discourse until noon, then stop for lunch, and then proceed to finish it. By three or four o'clock it was ready, and after a fair copy had been sent to Al it would be mimeographed for the use of the press.

Al's struggles with it were carried on *in camera,* so I can't report upon them in any detail, but there is reason to believe that he often made heavy weather of mastering his evening's argument. By the time he appeared on the platform he had reduced it to a series of notes on cards, and from these he spoke — often thunderously and always to the great delight of the assembled Democrats. But not infrequently his actual speech resembled the draft of the two judges only to the extent that the ritual of the Benevolent and Protective Order of Elks resembles the Book of Mormon and the poetry of John Donne. The general drift was there, but that was about all — and sometimes even the drift took a new course. The rest was a gallimaufry of Al's recollections of the issues and arguments in a dozen New York campaigns, with improvisations suggested by the time, the place and the crowd. It was commonly swell stuff, but I'd certainly be exaggerating if I said it showed any profound grasp of national issues. Al, always shrewd, knew that a Chicago crowd, or a rural Missouri crowd, or a crowd in Tennessee, Michigan or Pennsylvania did not differ by more than four per cent. from a New York crowd, so he gave them all the old stuff that he had tried with such success in his state campaigns, and it went down again with a roar. Never in my life have I heard louder yells than those that greeted him at Sedalia, Mo., in the very heart of the no-more-scrub-bulls country. His meeting was held in the vast cattle-shed of a county fair, and among the 20,000 persons present there were some who had come in by flivver from places as far away as Nebraska, Oklahoma, and even New Mexico. The subject of his remarks that night, as set by the two judges, was the tariff, but he had forgotten it in five minutes, and so had his audience. There were stenographers present to take down what he said, and transcripts of it were supplied to the press-stand sheet by sheet, but only a few correspondents actually sent it out. The rest coasted on the judges' draft, disseminated by the press associations during the late afternoon and released at 8 p.m., as he arose to speak. Thus all the Americans who still depended on the newspapers for their news — and there were plenty of them left in 1928 — were duped into accepting what the two laborious jurisconsults had written for what Al had actually said. I do not know, but the thought has often crossed my mind, that Hoover's overwhelming victory in November may have been due, at least in part, to that fact.

Al bore up pretty well under the rigors of the campaign, but now and then he needed a rest, and it was provided by parking his train on a side-track for a quiet night, usually in some sparsely settled region where crowds could not congregate. After his harrying of Tennessee, and just before he bore down upon Louisville to be fried, there was such a hiatus in rural Kentucky. When I turned out in the morning I found that the train was laid up in a lovely little valley of the Blue Grass country, with nothing in sight save a few farmhouses and a water-tank, the latter about a mile down the track. My colleague, Henry M. Hyde, suggested that we go ashore to stretch our legs, and in a little while we were hanging over a fence some distance to the rear of the train, admiring a white-painted house set in a grove of trees. Presently two handsome young girls issued from the house, and asked us prettily to have breakfast with their mother, who was a widow, and themselves. We accepted at once, and were very charmingly entertained. In the course of the conversation it appeared that another, daughter, not present, aspired to be the postmistress of the village behind the tank down the track, and Hyde, always gallant, promised at once that he would see Al, and get her a promise of the appointment come March 4, 1929.

When we got back to the train Hyde duly saw Al, and the promise was made instantly. Unhappily, Hoover won in November, and it seemed hopeless to ask his Postmaster-General to make good on Al's pledge. Four years of horror came and went, but the daughter down in the Blue Grass kept on hugging her ambition. When Roosevelt II was elected in 1932 her mother got into communication with Hyde, suggesting that the new administration should be proud and eager to make good on the promise of the Democratic standard-bearer four years before, even though that standard-bearer had since taken his famous walk. Hyde put the question up to Jim Farley, and Farley, a man very sensitive to points of honor, decided that Roosevelt was bound to carry out the official promises of his predecessor, however revolting they might be. An order was thereupon issued that the daughter be made postmistress at the water-tank at once, and Hyde went to bed that night feeling that few other Boy Scouts had done better during the day. But alas and alas, it turned out that the tank was a fourth-class post office, that appointments to such offices were under the Civil Service, and that candidates had to be examined. Farley so advised the widow's daughter and she took the examination, but some other candidate got a higher mark, and the scrupulous Jim decided that he could not appoint her. Hyde and I often recall the lamentable episode, and especially the agreeable first canto of it. Never in all my wanderings have I seen a more idyllic spot than that secluded little valley in the Blue Grass, or had the pleasure of being entertained by pleasanter people than the widow and her daughters. The place was really Arcadian, and Hyde and I wallowed in its bucolic enchantments while Al caught up with lost sleep on his funeral train.

He was, in his day, the most attractive of all American politicoes, but it would be going too far to say that he was any great shakes as an orator. Compared to Bryan he was as a BB shot to a twelve-inch shell, and as he was passing out of public life there was arising a rhetorician who was even greater than Bryan, to wit, Gerald L. K. Smith. As I have said, I have heard all the really first-chop American breast-beaters since 1900, and included among them have been not only the statesmen but also the divines, for example, Sam Jones, Gipsy Smith, Father Coughlin and Billy Sunday, but among them all I have encountered none worthy of being put in the same species, or even in the same genus, as Gerald. His own early training was gained at the sacred desk but in maturity he switched to the hustings, so that he now has a double grip upon the diaphragms and short hairs of the *Anthropoidea.* Add to these advantages of nurture the natural gifts of an imposing person, a flashing eye, a hairy chest, a rubescent complexion, large fists, a voice both loud and mellow, terrifying and reassuring, *sforzando* and *pizzicato*, and finally, an unearthly capacity for distending the superficial blood-vessels of his temples and neck, as if they were biceps — and you have the makings of a boob-bumper worth going miles to see and hear, and then worth writing home about. When I first heard Gerald, at the convention of the Townsend old-age pension fans at Cleveland in 1936, I duly wrote home about him to the *Sunpaper*, and in the following fervent terms:

His speech was a magnificent amalgam of each and every American species of rabble-rousing, with embellishments borrowed from the Algonquin Indians and the

Cossacks of the Don. It ran the keyboard from the softest sobs and gurgles to the most ear-splitting whoops and howls, and when it was over the 9000 delegates simply lay back in their pews and yelled.

Never in my life, in truth, have I ever heard a more effective speech. In logical content, to be sure, it was somewhat vague and even murky, but Dr. Townsend's old folks were not looking for logical content: what they had come to Cleveland for was cheer, consolation, the sweet music of harps and psalteries. Gerald had the harps and psalteries, and also a battery of trumpets, trombones and bass-drums. When he limned the delights of a civilization offering old-age pensions to all, with $200 cash a month for every gaffer and another $200 for the old woman, he lifted them up to the highest heaven, and when he excoriated the Wall Street bankers, millionaire steel magnates, Chicago wheat speculators and New Deal social engineers who sneered at the vision, he showed them the depths of the lowest hell. Nor was it only the believing and in fact already half dotty old folks who panted under his eloquence: he also fetched the minority of sophisticates in the hall, some of them porch-climbers in Dr. Townsend's entourage and the rest reporters in the press-stand. It is an ancient convention of American journalism, not yet quite outlawed by the Newspaper Guild, that the press-stand has no opinion — that its members, consecrated to fair reports, must keep their private feelings to themselves, and neither cheer nor hiss. But that convention went out of the window before Gerald had been hollering five minutes. One and all, the boys and gals of the press abandoned their jobs, leaped upon their rickety desks, and gave themselves up to the voluptuous enjoyment of his whooping. When the old folks yelled, so did the reporters yell, and just as loudly. And when Gerald, sweating like Al at Louisville, sat down at last, and the press resumed its business of reporting his remarks, no one could remember what he had said.

A few weeks later I saw him give an even more impressive exhibition of his powers. At the Townsend convention just described one of the guest speakers had been the Rev. Charles E. Coughlin, the radio priest, who, in return for Dr. Townsend's politeness in inviting him, invited the doctor and Gerald to speak at his own convention, scheduled to be held in Cleveland a few weeks later. But Gerald's immense success apparently sicklied him o'er with a green cast of envy, and when the time came he showed a considerable reluctance to make good. Finally, he hit upon the device of putting Gerald and the doctor off until the very end of his convention, by which time his assembled customers would be so worn out by his own rabble-rousing that nothing short of an earthquake could move them. On the last day, in fact, they were so worn out, for Coughlin kept banging away at them from 10 a.m. to 8 p.m., with no breaks for meals. The device was thus a smart one, but his reverence, for all his smartness, was not smart enough to realize that Gerald was actually an earthquake. First, old Townsend was put up, and the general somnolence was only increased, for he is one of the dullest speakers on earth. But then, with the poor morons hardly able to keep their eyes open, Gerald followed — and within five minutes the Coughlin faithful had forgotten all about their fatigues, and also all about Coughlin, and were leaping and howling like the Townsend old folks. It was a shorter speech than the other, for Coughlin, frowning, showed his itch to cut it off as soon as possible and Gerald was more or less uneasy, but it was even more remarkable. Once more the boys and gals in the press-stand forgot their Hippocratic oath and yielded themselves to pure enjoyment, and once more no one could recall, when it was over, what its drift had been, but that it was a masterpiece was agreed by all. When Gerald came to Cleveland it was in the humble rôle of a follower of the late Huey Long, jobless since Huey's murder on September 10, 1935. But when he cleared out after his two speeches it was in the lofty character of the greatest rabble-rouser since Peter the Hermit.

Coughlin, it seems to me, is a much inferior performer. He has a velvet voice, and is thus very effective on the radio, but like his great rival on the air, Roosevelt II, he is much less effective face to face. For one thing, he is almost totally lacking in dramatic gesture, for his long training at the mike taught him to stick firmly to one spot, lest the fans lose him in the midst of his howling. It is, of course, impossible for an orator with passion in him to remain really immovable, so Coughlin has developed a habit of enforcing his points by revolving his backside. This saves him from going off the air, but it is somewhat disconcerting, not to say indecent, in the presence of an audience. After the convention of his half-wits in Cleveland in 1936 a report was circulated that he was experimenting with a mike fixed to his shoulders by a stout framework, so that he could gesture normally without any risk of roaring futilely into space, but if he actually ever used it I was not present, and so cannot tell you about it.

A NOTE ABOUT THE AUTHOR

H. L. Mencken was born in Baltimore in 1880 and died there in 1956. Educated privately and at Baltimore Polytechnic, he began his long career as journalist, critic and philologist on the Baltimore *Morning Herald* in 1899. In 1906 he joined the staff of the Baltimore *Sun*, thus beginning an association with the *Sun* papers which lasted until a few years before his death. He was co-editor of the *Smart Set* with George Jean Nathan from 1908 to 1923, and with Nathan he founded in 1924 the *American Mercury*, of which he was editor until 1933. His numerous books include *A Book of Burlesques* (1916); *A Book of Prefaces* (1917); *In Defense of Women* (1917); *The American Language* (1918; 4th edition, 1936); *Supplement One* (1945); *Supplement Two* (1948); six volumes of *Prejudices* (1919, 1920, 1922, 1924, 1926, 1927); *Notes on Democracy* (1926); *Treatise on Right and Wrong* (1934); *Happy Days* (1940); *Newspaper Days* (1941); *Heathen Days* (1934); *A Mencken Chrestomathy* (1949); and *Minority Report* (1956). Mencken also edited several books; he selected and edited *A New Dictionary of Quotations* (1942). He was co-author of a number of books, including *Europe after 8:15* (1914); *The American Credo* (1920); *Heliogabalus* (a play, 1920); and *The Sunpapers of Baltimore* (1937).

Printed in the United States
57785LVS00004B/132